Welcome to

Mostly
^ True Reflections
on Fatherhood

Welcome to *Club Dad*

Mostly
^ True Reflections
on Fatherhood

George Jamison and Kenneth Freeston, Ph.D.

CompCare® Publishers

Minneapolis, Minnesota

Library of Congress Cataloging-in-Publication Data
Freeston, Kenneth Russell.
    Welcome to club dad: mostly true reflections on fatherhood/Kenneth
    Freeston and George Jamison.
        p. cm.
ISBN 0-89638-361-X
1. Fatherhood. 2. Parenting. I. Jamison, George. II. Title.
HQ756.F74 1994
306.874'2—dc20   94-37368
                                                                   CIP

Edit and interior design by Leah Peterson
Illustrations and cover design by Steve Michaels

Inquiries, orders, and catalog requests should be addressed to
CompCare Publishers
3850 Annapolis Lane, Suite 100
Minneapolis, MN 55447
Call 612/559-4800
or toll-free 800/328-3330.

To Kathy and Cheryl, whose contributions to this book, and to our lives, are too great to measure.

Contents

Siblings

Through a Child's Eyes

Time with Dad

About the Authors

Foreword

Two Fathers

Each of us goes through life with mental pictures of how we think our lives will be. Years of expectations and dreams shape our images. For many, the experience of having children emerges as a reality distinctly different from those pictures.

We are two men—as well as two fathers—writing about everyday experiences as seen from a father's point of view. George Jamison is dad to Simone and Bernadette and husband to Kathy. Ken Freeston is dad to David and husband to Cheryl. The surprises we encounter are many, but what surprises us the most is how much our children teach us every day, in quite ordinary ways. Many of their teachings are things we ourselves learned long ago.

As our children grow, they reawaken our own childhood experiences—long forgotten, yet very much alive. They find the hidden child in the adult.

Read. Smile. Think of the child within you.

Therapy for Daddy

Parents of small children have an exclusive health advantage that is rarely discussed or written about: the rejuvenating effects of exposure to youth. The medical journals never explore this phenomenon, but abundant proof of the dramatic effects of this scientific wonder are readily available. Take this morning, for example.

I woke up with an incredibly stiff neck. Actually, I knew it was stiff several hours before when, in the middle of the night, I rolled over and was awakened by the pain. Now that the sun was up, I found that even simple movements were painful and difficult.

Kathy, my wife, was sympathetic to my plight and asked how she could help comfort me. Her question went unanswered, because at that moment my daughter Simone arrived.

Simone is three years old. She loves her daddy, and every morning she wakes up anxious to see him. This morning was no different: she crossed the threshold of our bedroom in her usual manner, inquiring in one of her loud voices whether or not we were awake. Within moments she was on our waterbed, jumping her way toward the pillows where my head and sore neck were gently resting. Kathy immediately noticed my wincing and moaning and cautioned Simone.

"Be careful, Sweetie. Daddy's neck hurts."

She also noticed that Simone's grand entrance had awakened two-year-old Bernadette, and she set off to retrieve her from the crib. Now alone with Simone, I lay on my stomach unable to make any quick movements. I was at her mercy.

"Does your neck hurt, Daddy?"
"Yes, Honey."
"Can you move it?"
"No, Honey."
"Do you want me to kiss it?"
"Sure."

I had not anticipated that a kiss required an embrace. She grabbed my neck and pulled my head up toward her for a healing kiss. I saw stars.

"Is that better, Daddy?"

"Yes, it feels much better, Honey. Now, no more
kissing."

I eased over onto my back to enjoy Simone's smiling face.
The cheerful face of a three-year-old can't help but bright-
en your day, and Simone's big smile was doing just that.
Then I sensed a smaller, gentler presence. Bernadette had
arrived. Kathy asked Simone to come with her to the
kitchen for apple juice, which was served in plastic
Tupperware cups with spill-proof lids. They left.

Bernadette's large eyes and wide smile were like a tonic, helping me feel better by the moment. She decided to kiss me—
repeatedly. It was very sweet, and it warmed my heart to have
her cuddle next to my face, smiling and saying, "Daddy,
Daddy, Daddy." She tried to get closer to me. She repositioned herself by putting her small arm on my neck and leaning into it with her full nineteen pounds. I felt like the cartoon
character who got his tongue stuck in the light socket.

Simone then returned to save me.

"Be careful of Daddy. His neck hurts!"

The return of her sister filled Bernadette with new energy.

She grabbed my hair with both fists and yanked my head back and forth in rapid, jerky motions, yelling, "Daddy, Daddy, Daddy!" with each quick movement. Her beaming face was evidence that this clearly was fun.

The agony in my neck, while excruciating, didn't last long. Simone, who couldn't stand the thought of being excluded from all this action, leaped onto the bed and bounded toward us, landing straight on top of me.

Kathy could sense that this was becoming unpleasant for me and calmed down our two darlings. After a few minutes of relative peacefulness, my nerves had settled to a mild tingling. Bernadette decided to try removing the top from her juice. She succeeded and promptly spilled the cold liquid on my bare stomach. I flew into a sitting position, proving to myself that I was now capable of rising to face the day. Rarely have I been so eager to get out of bed on a Sunday morning.

A childless man may have stayed in bed half the day, nursing his pain and being coddled by his loving, attentive wife. Thanks to my daughters' therapy, however, I was on my feet and active within twenty minutes of waking. Life with two young children is never boring. That parental aphorism is true: children *do* help keep us young.

"Daddy, You Should Smile More Often"

Raising children is fraught with ironies. Before I became a parent, I often thought about what I would teach my children. I always said, "I'll never do this," or, "I'll always do that." But now that I actually am a parent, I find myself doing the very things my parents once did that I couldn't stand.

It's also frustrating for parents, new and old, to decide what to teach their children. I've spent my entire professional life as an educator, yet I have trouble knowing what to teach my child.

What values and beliefs do I want my son to hold? How can I help him make sound decisions, balancing his own desires with those held by others? How do I handle mistakes I make with him? What parts of my own upbringing do I relay to him, and what parts do I dump?

In David's early years, I remember extensively exploring and examining my past experiences. I had wanted to take the knowledge I learned (from my own hardships) and share it with him, so I could protect him from life's cruelties. The task, however, was far more difficult than I had imagined.

Children need time to be children and to live life for themselves. I have learned rather quickly that they will not believe a parent's word of caution until they have dabbled in "the forbidden." We can help our children make good decisions, but we cannot punish ourselves when they don't listen to us and are stuck with the consequences. One of the best teachers is firsthand experience.

On the other hand, children must not be pressured to behave as though they are adults. Too often parents place adult demands on children, forgetting that being a child is very serious stuff. There is a lifetime of adult experiences waiting for them. When they are young, they need to be children—and children only. I always thought that as a parent I would find the right balance in raising my children. And I thought I'd done a good job.

> Up until last week, that is, when my son, David, looked up at me and said, "Daddy, you should smile more often."

The truth of his statement was devastating. I considered myself such a conscientious father—I never even thought about being cheerful at the same time. In all my forty years, no one had ever told me this. From the mouth of my four-year-old came, simply and honestly, the best advice one person can give another. *Smile more often.*

This type of insight generally comes to an adult in life's twilight years, when the wisdom that comes with age causes reflection, nostalgia, and sometimes regret. People look back on life and think about how things might have turned out if only they had behaved or reacted differently. Only then do they become philosophers.

I have always known that learning is reciprocal, that teacher and student learn from each other. But why didn't I expect to learn from a small child? Did I underestimate his intelligence? When did I think I would start learning from him? When he was an "adult" at age eighteen?

There are dozens of answers, of course. Most parents believe that parents are parents and children are children, and parents show children how to do things.

This gives children security and safety, which they need in order to develop a peaceful, healthy self. However, this one-way pattern of authority lulls parents into the habit of being the provider, a pattern that can be quite difficult to break.

Being a parent takes on new meaning when the child is seen as the teacher. What can children teach parents? They can teach parents to

- ask questions,
- try new experiences,
- see things for what they are and be less analytical,
- and approach other people with trust and curiosity.

Adults often forget the exhilaration of discovery. We allow past experiences to limit new opportunities, and we think of ourselves as the answer-givers. In these ways and others we trap ourselves into a false sense of knowing it all (or at least most of it).

How often, when watching children play, do adults pine for the innocence and wonder of their own childhood? We see in children qualities we no longer have as adults. When, as adults, we have an experience that is "fun," why do we say, "I feel just like a kid again?"

Families gain unity when they believe that parents and children can learn from each other. When my son says, "This is how you do it, Mom and Dad," we are not surprised, and we don't tell David that he doesn't know how to do things. We try to do it his way. This gives him self-confidence and a sense of independence.

We do need the traditional parental roles to maintain order and ensure a solid upbringing, but we shouldn't forget that a most rewarding aspect of parenting is learning from our children.

Parents who love being parents know that children enrich adult lives. Children lessen life's burdens and offer optimism, enthusiasm, and curiosity. My son has taught me a very valuable lesson: I need to worry less and enter his world more fully *and smile more often.*

Who's in Charge?

Reveille

I know what profession my two daughters will choose as adults. They're perfectly suited for it; indeed, they have already refined some of the techniques that our government teaches to adults in special schools, to the tune of millions of taxpayer dollars. My little girls' dispositions are right for the job. Their wits are honed to precise specifications. They could qualify today as experts: *they are destined to be drill sergeants.*

Anyone who has spent so much as a day at boot camp or officer training school knows the prerequisites: a moody, volatile disposition; irrational thought processes; unbending devotion to senseless rules and traditions; and an attitude that embodies the phrase, "There are only two ways to do something: my way and the wrong way." Our children have mastered this.

Our bedroom door flies open every morning at precisely 0700, which is as late as our little sergeants ever let us sleep. Reveille is sounded.

"Jeeeeeeuiceee!!!"

That simple command means that Bernadette wants juice. The command is not answered instantly, which is reason for any drill sergeant to fly into a rage.

"Mommy, I want juice!!!"

"I'll get you some," I answered, in a valiant attempt to give Kathy a few extra moments of rest.

"No! Mommy!"

"I'll get the juice," I responded with authority in my voice.

Then the skirmish began.

"I want Mommy. I want Mommy. I want Mommy. I want Mommy."

Soon the storm subsided, and I offered Bernadette and Simone some breakfast.

"Daddy, I would like cereal," said Simone in a sweet, polite voice.

"One cereal coming up. How about you, Berna?"

"I would like cereal too," she replied.

As soon as I got the bowls out, they began to reconsider their selections.

"I want eggs, Daddy."

"I want that too."

"No, I want oatmeal."

"Can I have orange juice instead of apple juice?"

"Yeah, me too. I want orange juice."

"Do we have any lemonade?"

"Can I have some cheese?"

While I stood in the center of the kitchen dazed and confused, they mounted a frontal attack on the refrigerator.

"Oh, here's some yogurt!" Simone exclaimed.

"I want some too," Bernadette whined.

"There's only one, and I found it!"

"I WANT YOGURT!!!"

"Daddy, I found it first!"

Simone dashed for her chair, holding her yogurt like a football to prevent her sister from making off with it. Bernadette started grabbing random items from the refrigerator: cheese, jelly, mustard, horseradish.

"Wait a minute, girls!" I ordered, attempting to gain control. "The yogurt can be split, and we can have cereal, or eggs, or whatever else you want to eat."

"I don't want yogurt," said Bernadette.

"I can't share *this* yogurt," said Simone defiantly.

Upon hearing this, Bernadette decided that yogurt was the only food on earth that would satisfy her hunger. After much negotiation, both girls had yogurt, with cereal mixed in, and orange juice to wash it down. I finally sat down with my coffee. Bernadette came to sit on my lap, followed by Simone. Having arrived first, Bernadette positioned herself so that Simone could not climb on. As Simone moved to climb up my other leg, Bernadette repositioned herself to block her.

"Daddy, she won't let me get up!"

Bernadette grabbed my neck in a hammer lock to prevent any attempt to move her. Simone pushed Bernadette's leg. Bernadette slapped Simone on the top of her head. Simone slapped Bernadette's back. Bernadette began flailing her arms at her sister.

"Hey, stop this immediately!" I ordered.

Bernadette kept flailing.

14

"Bernadette, stop this right now, or I'll send you
  to your room!"

My youngest daughter looked at me with eyes wide open,
then her mouth puckered and twitched, her eyes watered,
and she burst into tears.

"Don't you say mean things to my sister," shouted
  Simone. "I'll send you to *your* room."

"But, but . . ."

"Come here, Berna," said Simone in soft, motherly
  tones. "Come on, let's go play in our room."

I was sitting in solitude when Kathy entered the room.

"What happened here?" she asked, with that
  gloating look on her face that said, "See what I
  go through every morning?"

Yogurt was splattered on the table. Juice was in puddles on
the floor. Miscellaneous items from the refrigerator were
scattered around the room. Cereal crunched underfoot.
The happy sounds of little girls at play were echoing down
the hallway.

"Oh, nothing. I just had a nice breakfast with
  the girls."

A Night with the Girls

Tonight Kathy was to attend a meeting, leaving me in charge of feeding, bathing, brushing hair, and putting our two daughters to bed. These are important duties that I take very seriously, and I was very happy to be entrusted with them. For a savvy dad like me, they would be routine and easy.

Oh, sure, there were a few snags, which began the moment I walked through the door, a bit late from work. Simone and Bernadette were in the process of eating a delicious meal of hot dogs, beans, bacon, and fruit. I'm a very lucky guy because my two daughters greet me like royalty every evening when I come home. Usually they stand at the top of the stairs screaming, "Daddy, Daddy," as I come up from the garage. I get big hugs and kisses, and they begin to tell me—both at once—about the highlights of their day.

Today, however, was different. The girls were well into their dinners when I came in, and so the routine took place in the kitchen with the two in their high chairs. When I say they were well into their dinners, I mean *physically*. Ketchup and bean sauce covered Bernadette's hands and arms up past the elbows. Her face was a reddish ball of ketchup with two eyes and a huge smile. Her juice had been spilled an inch deep on her tray, where it lay ready for splashing. There were beans on top of her head.

"Daddy!" she squealed with outstretched arms.

I got too close. She got my tie. Simone also demanded recognition. She was clean, and I gave her a hug.

> "I made a turkey at school today. Would you like to see it?" she inquired.
>
> "I sure would," I replied with enthusiasm, removing her from her high chair so she could go downstairs to the family room to retrieve it.

The Disney channel had been left on the television, and she never came back.

> "Bernadette has had her diaper off all afternoon and she's been going in the potty," Kathy explained.

I noted that the only articles of clothing Bernadette had on were an undershirt and socks. She was beaming with pride. Her mouth was crammed with hot dogs.

> "Gotta go," said Kathy. "See you in an hour."

As Kathy's car pulled out of the driveway, Bernadette started talking.

> "Daddy, my socks are wet."

They were indeed, and I don't think it was apple juice. As I peeled off her socks, she placed her little hand on my shoulder for support. Ketchup and bean sauce soaked into my shirt.

> "I want out," Bernadette insisted, lunging toward me.

She got me in a tight embrace, and I headed for the bath, hoping that she wouldn't squirm too much and spread her dinner completely over my clothes. I got the tub filled, put her in it, and called to Simone. She was in a hypnotic trance in front of the television.

> "Simone, it's time for your bath," I informed her.
>
> "Can't, Daddy," she said blankly. "I need to watch this; it's about a mouse."

Her logic made sense, but I couldn't give in too easily.

> "I think you'd better come now," I insisted.

She pleaded with me to let her watch the program. I pictured the usual squabbling, splashing, and fussing in the evening bath, and so I relented. She had my permission to watch the show while I bathed Bernadette. As I resumed my vision of two separate and peaceful baths for the girls, a scream filled my ears.

"BATH!!!"

"What?" I said, looking up to see Simone in the bathroom doorway.

"I need to have my bath now, with Bernadette."

Oh, now I understood. They bathed without incident, save the usual splashing of water out of the tub and onto the floor, walls, and innocent bystanders. I was even permitted to wash their hair without a struggle. I dried Bernadette and was in the process of drying Simone's hair when Bernadette informed me of a slight problem.

"My feet are wet!"

They were indeed. So were her legs and the floor beneath her.

"Bernadette, you're supposed to do that in the potty," I responded.

"Okay."

When everyone and everything were dry, I attempted to dress the girls for bed. Simone announced that she would wear her new pajamas, which were an exact match to the new pajamas we had also bought for Bernadette. The younger child, however, wouldn't hear of wearing her new jammies. When Simone returned from her room to see Bernadette in a nightgown, she began ripping off her own jammies. We could not find an exact match to Bernadette's

19

nightgown in Simone's dresser, which caused Simone great dissatisfaction.

While I was busy trying to appease her, Bernadette began flinging Simone's books from the book shelf into the middle of thc room. A struggle ensued, with swinging arms, piercing screams, and flying books. I threw myself in—suffering mild abrasions and several direct body blows.

Twenty minutes later, I had Bernadette in bed and Simone on my lap; we were peacefully reading a bedtime book. The garage door opened, and Kathy appeared.

"Everything okay?"

"Sure, no problem. It's nice to spend some quality time with the kids."

"Great," she replied. "I need to go out tomorrow night too."

Poops

When parents have their first child there is a great deal of interest in excrement. I have never understood why, but it seems to hold true. In fact, whole theories of personality development sometimes rely on how adults respond to the child's urge to poop.

My guess is that most parents remember their child's first poop. While the child is still in diapers, parents can tell from the face exactly when the diaper is being loaded. The face reddens, the eyes focus on something slightly above the horizon, and a small smile appears. In David's case, he always looked at us and said, "Hi."

When the first poop drops into a toilet, it is a big deal to everyone. What surprised us when this event happened was the deliberate way David got off the toilet, pulled a single section of toilet paper from the roll, and dropped it straight into the toilet.

Having observed us hundreds of times with curiosity, he had failed to notice the step in between the roll and the toilet. He simply thought that a flushed toilet always had to have toilet paper in it.

Another fact is that it is socially acceptable to talk about children pooping but rude and disgusting for the conversation to involve to adults. The only time it seems to be okay is when a person says, "I have the runs." Everyone has a clear picture of this, and the rest of the conversation is unspoken but quite complete.

Let's face it, diarrhea is not a pleasant experience. But when the toilet frequenter is a three-year-old, the events are somewhat different. David once had a bad experience with "the runs" and decided that this was not a great deal of fun. He was given a little of the medicine Mom and Dad take at such times, which he calls "peppo disney mall."

Poops and car trips do not mix well, although they always happen to children simultaneously. What parent hasn't embarked on an hour-long trip without hearing "I have to go to the bathroom" within the first ten minutes? Sometimes children may exaggerate their urgency in order to get attention. But not our David. He has always been accurate, which leads us to act reasonably fast because these proclamations are never spoken near a rest stop.

We learn from experience, his mother and I, and we now travel with a portable potty. A family hand-me-down from his cousins, it's a veteran model that has seen a lot of action. You almost expect to see bumper stickers on it. The first time we stopped at the roadside to use it was on the way to his grandparents' house on Cape Cod. David was fascinated with the idea of sitting on the toilet at the side of the road, and the idea worked well. No more searching for the next exit.

On the down side, children are distractible, and stops like this are likely to prompt questions. On a recent trip, Cheryl and David stopped for a roadside poop (David only). He spotted a butterfly and was not happy with Mom's orders to not run after it, pants down to the ankles. The longer they stayed, the more things David saw and the more questions he asked.

"What's that, Mommy?"

He pointed to a disgusting wad of paper and then offered his own imaginative answer. But eventually David went about his business, and the trip resumed.

By the way, the name of the upstate New York town where this occurred was *Deposit.*

On Our Best Behavior

My mother-in-law was visiting for two weeks from California, and as part of her east-coast orientation we took her on a tour of the Newport, Rhode Island, mansions. The entourage consisted of me, Kathy, my mother-in-law (known as Grandma Josephine), my sister-in-law Carolyne, and our two darlings, Simone and Bernadette.

We arrived at "The Breakers," former summer home of the Vanderbilt family, at about two-thirty in the afternoon. The children were well-rested from a two-hour nap in the car, and we were all anxious to get started with our tour of this famous attraction.

When purchasing our tickets, I took passing notice of a sign that read: "Children are most welcome. However, in consideration of our other visitors, disruptive children will be asked to leave the tour."

No matter, I thought, the children are on their good behavior today. We waited in line for twenty minutes or so.

> I should have sensed storm clouds on the horizon when our tour finally commenced and Simone asked, "Daddy, are we going to eat in there?"

Simone insisted on being carried; Bernadette couldn't make up her mind. Despite her insistence that she be alternately picked up and put down by each member of our party, Bernadette was relatively well-behaved through the first few ornate, gold-leafed, exquisitely furnished rooms.

An unfortunate pattern began to emerge at about the fourth stop on this twenty-room, hour-long tour. Bernadette was getting louder, more squirmy, and more ornery at each stop. The fifth stop was an open terrace, where photography was permitted and the children could run around harmlessly. I put the kids down, took in the glorious view, and savored the fresh, salty air. How I would long for this stop again later in the tour.

The trouble really began at the seventh stop, Mrs. Vanderbilt's bedroom. I was holding both children, and Bernadette insisted on setting off on her own. She was repeatedly yelling, "Let me down" and transforming herself into a fireball of kicking legs, flailing arms, and writhing torso.

I had broken a sweat at this point and wanted to quiet her down, so I honored her wish. She made a mad dash under the cordon rope toward the priceless artifacts and objets d'art that furnished the room. I got a hand on her before anything was damaged and glanced up to see a look of sheer horror on the face of our tour guide.

Frankly, I don't know what his problem was. I was the one at risk. A direct hit by "Hurricane Bernadette" probably would have caused enough damage to justify the seizure of my home, two cars, and entire salary for the next five to ten years.

Simone asked, "Are we going to eat in the next room, Daddy?"

Two stops later, in the grandly furnished recital room, Kathy had the idea of feeding the children mint candies from Grandma Josephine's purse. It worked—they were silenced! The tour group was quiet as our guide explained the acoustical merits of the room.

In a silent moment, Simone looked at me and said, "Daddy, I have to go to the potty."

The acoustics were indeed good. Bernadette decided to repeat her sister's phrase several times. As we progressed on our tour, her little voice resounded through the marbled halls.

"Daddy, I need to go to the potty!"

Simone asked, "Are we going to eat in this next room?"

By the time we reached the formal dining room, they had learned how to make noise with their mouths filled with mints.

Bernadette, who had squirmed down again, rushed under the ropes, this time toward a fountain in the large hall, proclaiming, "I want to get the water."

Simone grabbed my head with both hands, turned it so our noses were almost touching, and said, "Daddy, I need to go to the potty *now!*"

As we disappeared down the hallway to find the public rest rooms, I know the group heard Simone's voice echoing through the halls saying, "Daddy, are we going to eat when we get outside?"

I've heard that the breakfast nook, butler's pantry, kitchen, and flower pantry of the house are grand. I wouldn't know personally, because the remainder of my tour consisted of a visit to the public rest room, running around on the grass, playing with the stones on the pebbled driveway, and waiting for the group to catch up with us.

I do believe the highlight of the children's day occurred while waiting outside the gift shop, where they found three pieces of chewed and discarded gum stuck to a storm sewer grate.

"Whose gum is that, Daddy?"

"I don't know, girls, but don't touch it. We're going to eat soon . . ."

Wolves in Little Girls' Clothing

I am constantly amazed at the naiveté of childless adults. Now don't get me wrong. I'm not talking about those people whose children have grown and left the nest—those people are fully aware of the realities of life. I am talking about those people who merely grew up and went through adulthood without ever having children of their own. They are somehow deprived of the ability to glimpse the elements that form the foundations of humanity.

To be frank, they live in a dream world. When they see my two little daughters adorned in frilly dresses with their hair combed and their eyes bright, they see tiny adults. They envision how cute it must be to have these two charming creatures sit patiently at one's feet, politely listening to stories, their eyes wide with wonderment. In their mind's eye, they see peaceful dinners, where the little darlings use perfect etiquette while they calmly eat their meals, then cheerily trot off to a quick bath and bed.

Then, of course, the mother and father have coffee in the den. They will probably read or watch a little television, or maybe discuss politics, before retiring to bed for a blissful night's sleep, from which they will rise at a civilized hour to greet the children's smiling faces in the morning. To them I can say only one thing: these cute, huggable, darling little sweethearts have fooled you—they are wild animals in dresses!

For example, wild animals don't wear clothes, and they go to the bathroom wherever they please—just like Bernadette. At two years of age, Bernadette is very proud that she can dress and undress herself. She's really quite good at it. She'll choose her own clothes from her drawer and carefully dress herself, emerging in a purple shirt and pink shorts, both on backwards and not to be changed or adjusted in any way.

Later she'll tire of that outfit, shed those clothes somewhere in the living room, then go to her bedroom to select a dress from her closet. That will soon be found in the driveway, along with one shoe. Her third set of clothes are discovered in the bathroom, near the toilet, soaking wet from unknown causes. When we ask what happened, she'll either not remember or give us a brutally honest answer. I'm not sure which is worse.

Her behavior is equally uncivilized in public. Last weekend we went to pick strawberries at the local berry farm, and as we were standing in line to pay for our brimming basket of berries, Bernadette informed me that she had to go to the potty. I acknowledged her and said that as soon as we paid for the berries, I would take her.

The next thing I heard was some murmuring behind me, and as I turned around I saw that Bernadette had removed her shorts and underpants and was preparing to relieve herself. I quickly thrust the basket of berries into my wife's arms and scooped Bernadette up, trying in vain to get her shorts back on. We hustled over to a couple of port-a-johns near the trees, and I warned her before we entered that it might be a bit smelly in there.

I understated the condition, and as soon as we stepped inside she went into a frenzy, writhing and squirming frantically to get out of my arms. What she would have done with her freedom, had she gained it, is something I prefer not to speculate on. She was much happier going in the woods, as are most wild animals.

At the dinner table, Bernadette's manners are akin to Cheetah in an old Tarzan movie. She starts out very well, using her fork and spoon to get those first morsels of food into her mouth.

But as dinner progresses, the meal becomes more of an immersion experience. Baked beans are squashed with bare hands, then splattered about. A hamburger bun is wrung into a blob of dough, and the hamburger itself is shredded into individual strands of beef. Ketchup and mustard are smeared on the face, then the hands are cleaned on her shirt.

> "Daddy, I just ate a mosquito," Bernadette proudly informed me.

> Her mother, in a bold attempt at child psychology,

replied, "That's good Bernadette. Would you like to eat a few of these little fruit flies for dessert?"

Kathy offered her three small insects that were sitting on the Tupperware container. Don't ever do that.

Later we went out for soft ice-cream cones. It's funny how people think it's cute to see a small child who looks like a miniature Colonel Sanders with a melted ice-cream beard. Bernadette, of course, would not be wiped, yet she insisted on repeatedly hugging me. She got clean.

Simone, who is older, was proud that she was able to eat her ice cream without making a mess, and we praised her for doing so. Then a little cat came along to play. I noticed Simone petting the cat, then licking her hand, then petting the cat again.

"Simone, please don't lick your hand like that."

"Why?"

"Because you're petting the cat."

"But my hand is sticky."

"Then don't pet the cat."

"But he likes me."

"Yes, but he might be dirty."

"No, he's clean."

Somehow I thought that humans instinctively knew that furry animals may be dirty, and that licking sticky hands immediately after petting them was a bad idea. I was wrong.

The fact is that children must be taught virtually everything—how to walk, how to talk, how to share, how to control temper, how to behave around other human beings. Oh, sure, they pick up a few things on their own along the way, like dirty language and bad grammar. But for the most part there is little that comes automatically. Except one thing.

Children know how to love. My daughters can throw their arms around my neck and make me feel like the most important person in the world. And after their baths, they run to their room and ask for a story, then listen intently about the time my dad took me to a Yankees game, asking key questions like, "When Pop-Pop parked the car, was it between two other cars or was it by itself?"

And, come to think of it, when the children are finally in bed, Kathy and I do retire to the den with a cup of tea. . . and then pass out.

"Hi, Honey. I'm Home!"

An amazing thing happens to women who leave their careers to stay home and raise children: they discover the truth about their husband's work environment. These very same women who had their own "tough day at the office" stories in the prechild days are suddenly endowed with a new vision, a new sense of truth.

It happens slowly at first, in a step-by-step process during the first few months of staying home with the infant. Gradually the facade of a man's life in the office is peeled away, layer by layer, like the outer skins of an onion. Then, one day, the final truth strikes like a lightning bolt, and the new mother's eyes are opened.

Men go to their offices to luxuriate, and escape the duties of fatherhood, while assistants dash about catering to their every whim.

From that point on, the sham is pitifully transparent. A late night at the office is clearly a plot. Even his boss and coworkers stay late to help him avoid feeding the baby and putting the tyke to bed. Indeed, the very act of leaving for work in the morning is a paper-thin excuse to stick his wife with all the child-rearing work.

In all fairness, let's face it, staying home with small children is no picnic. In fact, when done properly, it is unquestionably one of the most challenging, exhausting, and thankless jobs around. Men know this.

This presents the father of young children with a dilemma. He can work late every night, but sooner or later he must go home. He's in a delicate spot, because he has no idea what he'll find when he opens that front door.

In an effort to help my brothers in fatherhood, I have scientifically categorized three main scenarios that fathers encounter upon returning home from work. The scenarios are characterized by the attitude of the mother and vary in intensity. I hope they'll prove useful to fathers in preparing for the ensuing years.

Level 1: "Hi, Honey. Welcome home!"

The house is orderly, the aroma of dinner floats from the kitchen, and the children are sleeping or quietly watching television. They've had a pleasant day without any turmoil or excessive excitement. Everyone is in a good mood. Note: this is a rare occurrence and will probably not be encountered often with children under three years of age.

Level 2: "Thank goodness you're home. Now you can take care of these kids for a while."

Probably the most common occurrence. If you have an infant child, your wife will immediately accomplish a maneuver called "the hand-off," which involves thrusting the baby—often with some degree of force—into your arms. Grab the child tightly and hold securely; your wife has no intention of taking the child back anytime soon.

The older children will be playing noisily, running around, and probably screaming. If you have two or more children, one will be crying or show evidence of a recent tantrum. Toys are scattered about. Dinner is thawed but not yet in the oven. At least one broken item is on the kitchen counter waiting to be glued. All in all, it's been an average day.

Level 3: "Don't you dare be in a good mood. These children are all your fault. I've suffered all day. Now it's your turn."

This is the dread of every father, and it requires extreme caution. Your first action is to survey the area carefully. Evidence of disaster is everywhere.

Food is splattered all over the kitchen. The bathroom floor is covered with water, and the toilet is clogged with towels. Streams of toilet paper trail through the house. Toys are strewn about everywhere, especially on stairways. The air is thick with noise from the TV, radio, washing machine, and screaming children. The countertop holds several items waiting for glue. At least one child sports a bandage, and clothes litter the hallway.

Do yourself a favor: don't even go near the couch!

This situation requires immediate action. First, get to the phone. If it's still working, call the closest pizza restaurant and order a family special to go. Do not have the food delivered. Get the children in the car and go pick up the dinner, leaving Mom at home alone. Play games with the kids, calm them down, hug them. Use a combination of threats and bribes to ensure their good behavior at dinner. Pick up a special treat for Mom, and make sure the kids give it to her.

Remember, this is the easy part. Someday they'll be teenagers.

Creaking Floors, Sleeping Children

There are not many sights more humorous than a forty-year-old father crawling out of a sleeping toddler's bedroom. On my knees, moving one hand at a time, I try to leave the room without making a sound. Putting a child to bed will challenge even the most assertive and confident parent.

How do parents decide how to parent? The ideas come from a variety of sources and experiences, some from the way parents were treated as children, some in opposition to the way they were treated. Some parents talk to other parents and friends, exchanging ideas and frustrations. Still others consult child-development experts.

Bookstores carry shelves of books advising parents on how to be parents. Today one can read about every conceivable child behavior and appropriate parent response. Experts offer techniques to raise intelligent, well-adjusted, socially conscious, healthy children.

But those who write about putting a child to bed stress the importance of letting children learn how to put themselves to sleep. In doing so, they learn independence. They sleep better. And bedtime is less of a nightly power struggle. These ideas all make perfectly good sense to me.

I end up reading a dozen or so books until I find an expert who agrees with me, and then I decide that this is the one I will follow. The question is this: how do you convince an active, fully alert child that the day is over and that he or she must find a way to fall asleep? To a small child, routines—especially bedtime routines—are important. They provide security and give children an understanding of something they can depend on every night. (They also provide the early development of extraordinary negotiation skills.)

In our family, the nightly routine starts with a bath. Then the fun begins. We sit in Grandma's front porch rocker and read stories, sing songs, talk about the day, and dream about the future. We call this time together "rock-rocks." These are the best times of the day; I will miss them terribly when David grows up. For now, however, I can look forward to spending quality time with my son until it is time for him to go to bed.

Although he can't tell time yet, David knows when it is his bedtime, so he starts his negotiations early in the evening. Children can be very goal-directed, especially when the objective is to *not* go to bed. After dinner David usually will make us chase him around to get him into the bathtub. As his secondary tool of procrastination, he then prolongs his bath—which he didn't want to take in the first place. In the tub, a second series of stalls can buy at least an extra half hour.

Once David is in his pajamas, he comes up with an endless supply of "one mores." One more book, one more glass of water, one more stuffed animal in the bed, one more stuffed animal out of the bed.

The left brain says, be in control, don't negotiate, don't be manipulated, set limits, and myriad other phrases to avoid raising a spoiled, controlling, obnoxious child. Then I think about how little this child actually does control. I think about how important it is for him to get what he wants sometimes so he learns there is a reward for being persistent. After all, bedtime is fairly arbitrary. So I stay with him another ten minutes, and he falls asleep.

Don't let anyone misinform you—there are few things in life more fulfilling than watching a sleeping child. Every parent knows this feeling. It is more addictive than moving water or falling snow. I am not sure why. I suppose, in part, it's a feeling of accomplishment. Perhaps it is because we have all made it through another day, or perhaps it's a nostalgic passage to our own childhood nights. Selfishly, it's the arrival of the first free time of the day to be a person, not a parent, not a professional.

Sleep, however, is often an illusion. The routine has one more step: leaving the room without waking the child. There are toys to trip over—things that squeak, and even some that have minds of their own. My son can sleep through thunderstorms, doorbells, and barking dogs, but at this point every night the slightest sound can often snap up his eyelids. Over by the door there is a floorboard that creaks. I think it moves too, because it's never in exactly the same place. If I step on it, he wakes up. One time the floor was quiet, but my ankle bone clicked. His eyes opened.

"Where arc you going, Daddy?"

Some Assembly Required

Before I became a father, I thought that assembling a barbecue grill was the ultimate challenge for any consumer who braves a purchase that has to be put together. I had assembled four grills in my lifetime, ranging from a cheap charcoal model fifteen years ago to a top-of-the-line gas model two years ago. I completed them all, despite missing parts, skinned knuckles, and vows never to assemble *anything* again.

I am not a klutz. I tackle projects around the house all the time. Actually, I enjoy it, especially if I do not have to follow someone else's directions. The basement workbench is well-stocked with tools, old and new. In our world of uncertainty and ambiguity, there is something rewarding about taking a project from start to finish. I have built decks and outdoor sheds, refinished furniture, and completed many other fairly impressive projects.

After becoming a father, however, I started shopping for toys.

There is a particular night in late December when many parents *assemble.* My first disaster came on such a night. The toy was a five-foot plastic tree house that stood on four orange legs, had a green roof, blue stairs, and a slide. It was a popular model, one that nearly every toy store sold.

I like to reduce the failure odds by purchasing a major brand name—which this was—with clear instructions. Most assembly directions are written for klutzes, and as a nonklutz, I figured I was at an advantage. When I saw the pictures of the three tools I needed, under the "some assembly required" warning, I felt confident. After all, if there was a picture of a screwdriver on the outside of the box, how difficult could it be?

It was a cold December night, and by the time I began, the family room thermostat was already on the night setting. Two hours later, my sweater, shirt, and turtleneck were off; I was dripping with sweat, and the tree house was but one step away from completion. All I had to do was attach the four orange legs. Then I read the last line in the directions: "This may require considerable pressure."

I weigh over two hundred pounds. But even jumping from the fireplace ledge with samurai-like movements did not accomplish the task. Because I am an insistent perfectionist, this bothered me.

There ought to be a school somewhere that teaches people to write assembly instructions. I have two graduate degrees and consider myself to be an intelligent person, but few documents are more regularly puzzling to me than instructions intended to help me put something together. People do not learn the art of understatement like this on their own. And how about those "illustrations," the simple line drawings showing the progression of tasks that purport to lead to the picture on the outside of the box? I often wonder if the people who draw the pictures and write the instructions ever try to build the thing in the first place. Anyway, I finally got the project assembled, no thanks to the instructions.

Remembering that night, I was more cautious the next December. A good friend and veteran of many Christmases gave me a tip: assemble early.

How complicated could a small tricycle be? Now a wiser shopper, I priced the model I wanted at several stores and settled for one of those catalog places where you look at a picture of the item, write down its number, and wait an hour for the thing to arrive on a conveyor belt.

A week before Christmas, I opened the box and encountered the first obstacle: wrong tricycle. Calmly, I decided this was not a problem. I simply took it back and got the right one to come along the conveyor belt. Home again, I quickly got to the last two assembly steps when I hit my second obstacle: a missing part. Back to the conveyor belt.

This is not an uncommon problem; people everywhere can identify with it. In fact, it happens so often that parents can finish the details of the experience for each other. By this time, I was worried that the trike might be out of stock. Luckily, it was still available. I checked to be sure it was the right one—with all its parts—before I left the store for the third time.

That night I read about the notion of "zero defects" and other aspects of the quality sciences, now popular with people who strive to improve American business. There is wisdom in the idea that people will pay more for quality. I certainly will. How does Santa manage to build all those toys, every year, with missing parts and unreadable instructions?

David's fourth Christmas will be unique. There will be no back orders, no batteries, and—not surprisingly—no assembly required. Thank you, Santa.

Eight Lessons for Christmas

Last year on Christmas afternoon, I promised myself that I would remember several lessons when I paced the malls in future years in search of gifts for my little girls.

Lesson 1: Size determines perceived value.

One cannot underestimate the importance of size when selecting gifts for young children. Careful study has shown that children will touch, shake, examine, and ponder large packages far more frequently than small packages during the pre-Christmas period. Gifts that come in boxes large enough to play in provide an extra bonus because large boxes inevitably become the toy of choice later in the day, after all of the expensive toys break or the batteries wear out.

Lesson 2: Toys count more than clothes, by several orders of magnitude.

My two girls love their clothes. They debate endlessly with us over the clothes they'll wear on any given day. They know exactly what's in their closet and have definite feelings about which clothes are appropriate for specific events. All this aside, expensive little dresses and outfits are immediately dropped to the floor the moment the wrapping paper is removed from the box. But a cheap plastic toy will be showered with attention all morning and late into the day.

Lesson 3: Only parents appreciate technical sophistication.

Barbie's soda fountain, with all of its thousands of nearly microscopic parts, is enjoyed at its lowest level of sophistication. Only Dad bothers to learn—or even wants to know—how to set it up and use it. The girls just want to take all the little pieces for a ride in the stroller, put them in their mouths, and lose them as quickly as possible.

Lesson 4: Wrap the gifts well—most of the fun is in the opening.

An opened present is an uncovered secret. No matter how good the gift is, the allure is lost upon opening. As long as plenty of wrapping paper covers the gift, the child's awe and fascination remain.

Lesson 5: Take careful note of who gives what to the children.

Efficiency is paramount to young children opening presents. Their minds are locked in a shredding mode, causing them to tear paper furiously and forcefully from packages in a frantic quest to discover the contents. Parents can help by remembering whom to thank.

Special note: the children will be happy to open their presents, your presents, the dog's and cat's presents, and any wrapped parcel within sight. They can't read the tags, so they proceed with immunity. They can open an amazing number of gifts in a short period of unsupervised time.

Lesson 6: It is possible to have too much.

Last year our children were drunk with presents. They became numb after an hour or so of clawing and tearing at wrappings. Moderation is a virtue often neglected at Christmas.

Lesson 7: Don't waste your breath giving the moderation speech to grandparents—they don't want to hear it.

And besides, who am I to put limits on the pleasure they get from shopping for, wrapping, and giving presents to their grandchildren? Of course—grandparents, take note—we may need a larger house soon.

Lesson 8: Savor every moment.

The holidays hold great magic for children—Santa Claus, reindeer, elves, stories, candy, cheer. The holiday spirit changes and often diminishes as we get older. Although this remains a special time of year, somehow going to bed on Christmas Eve is just not the same after you've learned the sad truth: jolly old Saint Nick doesn't really come down the chimney, and if someone actually tried to slither down your chimney, he'd be bitten by the family dog and hauled off to jail.

All of that spirit returns when you have children in the house. Santa and his elves become more than department store decorations; they reside back at the North Pole once again. The story of Mary, Joseph, Jesus, and the three wise men becomes new and fresh again. Decorating the tree becomes more of a celebration than a chore. We sing more carols, eat more food—and give more hugs.

Most of us weren't born with enough wisdom to savor these moments as children. Now, as parents, they will slide past us again. We must enjoy them to the fullest.

The Child in the Man

On the way to Roberto-the-Barber's to have his hair cut for the second time, David started to wiggle, and a look of discomfort and uncertainty came over him.

"Daddy, I don't want to go to Roberto's today."

I could see he was really disturbed, so we didn't go.
The next weekend the same thing happened. David was three, and I was not eager to start a pattern of hated trips to the barber shop.

"Why?" I asked.

"Because I don't want him to put that cape on me."

I thought of my own childhood haircuts in Berkeley Heights, New Jersey. The four chairs in a straight row made of red leather and chrome seemed huge at the time, especially when the barber jacked the chair even higher. I recall the sensations of the electric trimmer and the pieces of needle-sharp hair it left on my neck. In front of me, black combs stood on end in a jar filled with blue liquid. On the counter, a poster of the perfectly trimmed big toenail leaned against the mirror. It showed how to avoid an "ingrown toenail." I had trouble visualizing this ailment and wondered why the poster about toes was in a barber shop in the first place.

I decided I'd try to help David overcome his fear of barber shops.

> "We'll ask Roberto," I said, "if you can leave the cape off, but you will have to keep your hands on your lap."

Roberto said fine, and I continued to think about haircuts I'd had as a little boy. I remember how compliant I was with the barber, how much power I let him have over me. Authority is unpredictable in a child's life. David complies with Roberto's slightest requests, while there are other people, like his parents, whom he frequently ignores.

I remember how still I sat in the chair, the way the barber (his name was Gus) pushed my ear toward the front as he trimmed with the scissors. The thick yellow lotion he used to stiffen my hair left me with a lingering smell for the rest of the day. I returned to David. His head was motionless as he tried to look from side to side with his eyes. His two little hands clutched the cloth of his pants.

Often David summons my own childhood experiences buried deep within my memory. Something insignificant that happens in his day triggers a part of my own past, which I then recall in vivid detail. Some psychologists call this collection of memories the "inner child." Today anxiety often enters my life when I am in situations that call for adult behavior, leaving me to conclude that, even now at age forty, I have a healthy, active child inside me.

David's experiences reawaken my childhood memories of Berkeley Heights. There is little known about this place, aside from its being the hometown of Mary Jo Kopechne, and you had to live there to know this. We moved there in 1956, and we left in 1962. Six years. Yet, through my son's life now, I recall details of those years that are still very much a part of me: the house, my room, the yard, the neighborhood, and my bicycle, which I rode at dusk after supper on summer nights.

It was a time when houses were first being built with Sheetrock instead of plaster, and plywood instead of pine boards. A suburban town, one that opened street after street of new split-level homes, offered adventurous play for kids in the 1950s. They gave rapt attention to building crews and construction equipment—and they couldn't wait to explore the wooden frames and foundation holes when the workers went home. Discarded scraps filled my bike basket—as they became valuable "things" to take home to my own backyard.

I remember my backyard swingset, the motion, the rhythm, the exhilaration. New suburban swingsets were metal then, replacing the wooden ones of earlier days. Corner stakes never quite did the job of keeping the frame from wobbling; this provided an incentive for swinging higher. The seat was flat, red metal, unlike the smooth, curved rubber seat at the school playground.

The world of play opens up when a child learns to pump on a swing, to be independent from the need to be pushed. David swings on a wooden swing, which has now replaced the metal swing (which replaced the wooden swing). As I watch him struggling to learn how to pump, I remember how I tried to swing up even with the top support bar, not accepting that you really can't swing all the way around it, full circle. Eyes closed, I surrendered to the rhythm and thought of what life would be like as a big kid, feeling the wild anticipation of growing up. Then I would open my eyes and drag my feet in the dusty hollow below, shaped by the endings of previous rides.

These thoughts raced quickly through my mind as my son got his hair cut. I watched him. He looked into the mirror and studied his own face. This must be something that happens during every haircut, I suppose. That seemingly insignificant fifteen minutes each month presents time to reflect on haircuts past, on experiences past. As he gazed at his face in the mirror, I wondered what was going through his head while Roberto snipped and combed his fine, blond hair. Was he thinking about his future as I was thinking about my past?

All parents worry about a child's future. Will David grow up to be a happy, self-assured person, one who cares about himself, other people, and the environment? Will his developing inner child enrich his adult life? Even more significant is the reality that my daily actions help shape his future.

In this country, we believe that healthy families have good parent-child relations. While this is certainly true, why is it that our best times as father and son are those times when I am a child too?

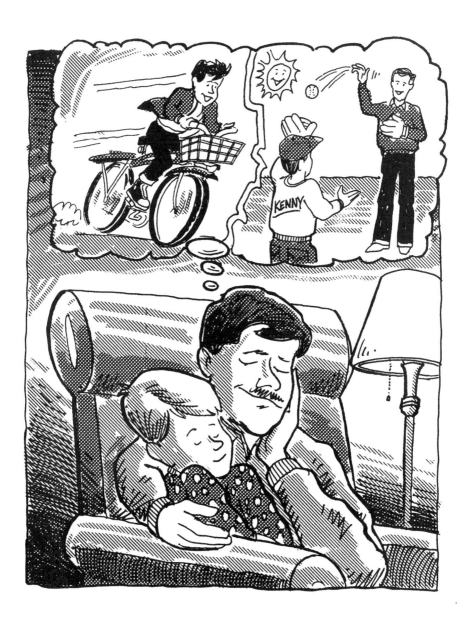

Front Porch Rocking Chairs

When I go on a vacation, I drop out. I like to escape the pressures of responsibility and decision making and revel in the choice to do nothing.

Not surprisingly, I take my family to the summer vacation spot where I went as a child: Long Lake Village. I am told there aren't many places left like this. The Larson family runs the place—the fourth generation of Larsons, actually. They built the main villa themselves around 1900 and each of the nineteen lake houses in later years.

We have gone there as a family for five summers; most families there have made the same trip for at least twenty years, the same week each summer. Many of the guests are second- and third-generation visitors. There's a waiting list to get in, and the Larsons haven't advertised the village in eighty years. Even more surprising, people line up to pay their bills a day early.

Why is the place so special? For many of the guests, part of the appeal is the Larson family itself. In today's world of large resorts and corporate rates, Long Lake Village stands proudly and quietly as an example of the way things once were.

Business is conducted with a handshake. There are no televisions or phones in the rooms. The doors have no locks. At the boathouse, in the villa, or around the grounds there are always some Larson family members talking with the guests about weather, kids, and maple syrup.

Not much changes. This year there was new wallpaper in the dining room, and that is about as big as the changes come. No one talks about careers or world events, though I expect great discussions could develop. Instead, people rock on front porch rockers and talk of summers past. The same people come each year, so there's always some catching up to do.

During the day, some golf, swim, or play tennis. At night people play bingo and dance the "alley cat." But the peace that comes from a Long Lake Village front porch rocking chair is like none other.

There must be a hundred of these rocking chairs. Each one is painted in bright, primary colors and has a view of the lawns that stretch to the lake below. The rush seats show the contours of earlier generations. In fact, these chairs are so much a part of the villa, the Larson family sends a picture of them empty on their Christmas cards.

People generally sigh and smile when they have their first rock of the year. David, at age four, does not fully appreciate the sedentary joys of this type of holiday. Sitting in a rocking chair is not his idea of a summer vacation. For him, each day at Long Lake Village is packed with activity. We start at 7:30 A.M. with a walk to the villa for breakfast.

On the way we watch Scotty and Hank groom the tennis courts. After breakfast the children go to the playhouse for the morning, a sort of parentless play group to give the moms and dads some adult time.

David has a clear idea of the events to follow. This is good—he's very future-oriented. BUT, the trouble with this approach is that his list of future events and mine often are not the same.

After lunch he plays tennis, goes to the beach, and then putts on the putting green before dinner. Playing tennis with a four-year-old is more exhausting than you would think. He is barely as tall as the net, but he can hit a drop serve the full length of the court. While he hits, I roam around picking up yellow balls.

Firm in his belief that he can't get his face wet and still live, David spends most of his time at the beach inventing ways to get wet without letting water ever touch his face. No matter how many times I dunk my head under, he still doesn't believe that I will survive the next time.

On the putting green he prefers to use my two iron, the longest club in the bag. The guests smile sympathetically and say something like, "You can't start them too young."

After dinner there's shuffleboard, more tennis, and the first warnings from me that bedtime is near. Once—after a string of action-packed days—David fell asleep at dinner. Right in the dining room. The possibility that I could have an evening to do nothing was at hand. I carried him out of the dining room and back to the house, eyeing the rocking chair where I would soon land. I had first seen it on the Christmas card eight months earlier.

While I was changing him into his pajamas, he moved slightly. I had been caught. With eyes half open, he realized that the day was ending for him earlier than he had planned. He started to cry—pout, actually—the kind of cry that starts with the quivering lower lip.

"Daddy," he said, "I didn't get a chance to slide down that dirty place."

There's always one more thing for a kid to do before going to bed, but on vacation the temptations are more exhilarating and urgent. I never really found out where the dirty place was, but at that moment it was very important to him.

At the end of days like this, I look back at those front porch rockers and think about the tranquillity that comes with being perched there for a bit of time.

I then say to myself, "Maybe next year."

Once a Banzai, NOT Always a Banzai

Each summer a carnival comes to town. I just recently realized why we go. It's one of those traveling amusement parks with dinky—yet frightening—rides set up for a week. The rides, lights, sounds, and people create an aura of excitement for kids. But that is not why we go.

We go for the cotton candy.

Psychologists and learning theorists describe categories of behavior to help explain the different actions we choose in the same situations. Somewhere there should be a description of carnival styles, a listing of the specific ways kids behave in amusement parks. Here is my contribution.

At one end of the spectrum is the banzai kid. When this reckless warrior charges into the park, he breaks away from Mom and Dad and at a full gallop races toward the most frightening ride. This pace does not stop, ever. You can pick out the parents of banzai kids by the woozy, pale expressions on their faces. I know, because I was a banzai kid.

At the other end of the spectrum is the groper. Groper behavior is characterized by rapt attention to all that happens, but from the perspective one gets while being held by a parent. The parents of groper kids do a lot of pointing and suggesting.

Over time, I think most kids change from gropers to banzais. David's first carnival signaled his preference for groping—two hours of walking around without a single ride! There was, however, immediate engagement whenever we passed the food stands. I think kids are genetically attracted to cotton candy. Or maybe enthralled at the sight of a bag of candy bigger than their teddy bear. How can a child even think about eating something that looks so big?

The stuff is laced with what I call *carnadisiacs,* tiny sugar drugs that give kids the urge to ride. After David ate his first bag of cotton candy (or smeared it on his face and hands) he pointed to a small rotating ride, the kind that has stationary cars and occasional buzzers. He had made his first step toward being a banzai.

Cotton candy's drug-like qualities also must be addictive. It was the first thing he wanted when we returned to the carnival the next year. And the effects were relatively the same. Only the lights were brighter and the rides more alluring.

When we were preparing to go for the third year, it was the only thing he talked about doing before we got there.

In fact, when we woke up that morning, he bolted upright in bed and said, "Today we get cotton candy," with his right arm stretched out fully and fist clenched.

The third year was the turning point in his conversion from a groper to a banzai. I saw it happen when he went on the jumping thing. David names each ride in a fairly logical fashion. There's the turning thing, the spinning thing, the sliding thing, and, of course, the jumping thing.

We started the night at one of the turning things—six tired vehicles turning slowly on a disk under a brightly colored canvas top. Lights were flashing and buzzers sounding. The vehicles were doing nothing, so this was a perfect first ride for a groper. After making the rounds to some of the other rides, David spotted the cotton candy, but on his own he decided to wait a little longer. However, just the sight of the pink blob gave him confidence to go on the jumping thing.

This was one of those large, circular, air-filled pillows with a cloth roof and netting around the outside. The air cushion was three-feet thick, and it was constantly being recharged by a gas-powered air pump. Through the netting parents watched bobbing, running, and jumping preschoolers, squealing with delight. Actually, this was better than the rides because the children do the moving, instead of being spun, turned, and sped by a machine.

There was David, timid on his first try, amid the dozen or so banzais. But he had an expression on his face that said, "I think I could get to like this." Then, like Popeye to spinach, we went to the cotton candy. He was with his friend Nicky, and they loaded up. While the sugar coated the inside and outside of their bodies, Nicky's Mom and I went on the Rock-O-Planes. It was the double-action kind where you sit in cages, in pairs, and spin in a full circle while the wheel itself rotates. How bad could it be, especially for a couple of seasoned banzais?

Shortly into the ride it occurred to me that I had made a terrible mistake. Although this ride was a banzai's delight, for the first time in my adult life I realized I was no longer a banzai. Growing older meant returning to groper status! On one of the spins I noticed far below that Nicky and David had finished the cotton candy and were confidently headed back toward the jumping thing.

> "You look green, dear," Cheryl said when Katie
> and I got off the ride.

And there, through the netting, I saw David's head bopping up and down, his little body darting fearlessly around the air cushion. Had I passed on to him my banzai spirit—like a baton—during the ride, or was it the magic of cotton candy?

Later that night, I thought about the events of the evening. David was in his room with Cheryl, bubbling with stories of the night's fun. I was flat in bed, still faintly green, waiting for my stomach to settle from the humbling experience.

A banzai never wants to admit that the ride won. Next time, maybe if I eat some cotton candy just beforehand . . . .

As Quickly as Tomorrow

Last Saturday my friend Jack strolled down the church aisle with his eldest daughter's arm tucked in his own, giving her away in marriage. The young groom was from a different city in a different state, and Jack probably hasn't spent more than a total of five hours in his company. I think he was happy, but Jack had a distinct passion in his voice last week at lunch when he looked at me and commented that it seemed like only yesterday that his daughter of twenty-something years was just a baby.

I believe it. Four years, five months, and three days ago, I stood in a hospital corridor staring down into the tiny, new face of my first daughter. I will never forget her irregular breath and her dark eyes, which were blinking slowly and taking in the new sensation of light. *That* was only yesterday, yet it seems I can barely remember the time before we had children.

I haven't slept past 8:00 A.M. in years, nor have I sat down on a Sunday afternoon to enjoy a good book. My feet have become impervious to the cold, wet, squishy things they encounter when I walk into the kitchen on a Saturday morning after my daughters have been eating their breakfast. My audio reflexes have dulled to the constant banging, screaming, crashing, pounding, crying, and slamming noises that thunder down our hallway when the girls are playing in their bedroom. In fact, it's become fun to contrast the darting eyes and nervous glances of childless adults with the relative calm of battle-hardened parents, who seem not to hear the inevitable noises of destruction that emanate from any group of children hard at play.

Simone and Bernadette have personalities so distinct, so flamboyant, so lively, that I feel they've been with us much longer than four-and-a-half years.

Kathy cried when we moved baby Simone from the bassinet in our bedroom to the crib in her own room. I was excited, quite frankly, and couldn't understand why she was sad. But she may have realized that this was the first, small move in the momentum that would take Simone evermore quickly into adulthood and away from us.

Sometimes when I look at our daughters' faces, beaming each day with the pride of some small but significant achievement, I wonder what they'll be like in twenty years.

Will they maintain the same bright outlook and passion for living that fills them now, or will life pound some of that out of them? Will they reach high to strive for their full potential, or will they turn their backs and let moments of decision pass them by while they amuse themselves with distractions? Will I be able to create an atmosphere they can thrive in and set an example that is worthy of following?

I don't know the answers to these questions, but I do know one thing: I've decided that I must live their childhood with them. I cannot, and will not, become too preoccupied to listen to their stories or to tell them stories when they want to hear them. I've got to take time to play with them on their swingset and help them catch toads in the yard. I must put down the mail or turn away from the news to watch when they want to show me something. If I don't, they'll keep growing anyway, but they'll learn to do it out of my sight.

And when the day comes that I walk my daughter down the aisle, I'll be able to look over at her and know I did my best to share in every aspect of her life.

I'm sure it will come as quickly as tomorrow.

Dad Always Liked You Best

My children's needs are simple—each of them needs what the other child has. The rule applies evenly and universally, from the selection of lunch through preparation for bed.

> "Simone, what would you like for lunch?" I asked innocently.
>
> "What's Bernadette having?"
>
> "I don't know yet."
>
> "Then I want a sandwich."

"What kind?"

"Are you having cheese? I want cheese."

She ate her selection happily at the table, until Bernadette arrived.

"I want peanut butter and jelly," announced the younger one.

Simone was immediately activated.

"I want peanut butter and jelly too," she said, her mouth stuffed with cheese.

Bernadette then asked to sit in the booster seat. Without hesitation, I obliged.

"No, I want the booster seat," whined Simone, causing Bernadette to beam in triumph from her perch.

Simone began to climb the chair, and Bernadette put up her guard, grabbing handfuls of Simone's hair and screeching. I ended the fight, ordering Simone back to her place at the table while Bernadette remained, victorious, on her throne. But nature soon called my younger daughter, and I got her down so she could go to the potty.

Simone, of course, seized the opportunity and dashed for

the booster seat, but Bernadette, who's no fool, answered this naked aggression with the ferocity of a mother bear separated from her cub.

> "Simone, go back to the table," I sternly demanded. "Bernadette, go to the potty, and don't worry, I won't let Simone take the seat."

My credibility must have been lacking, because Bernadette lingered, watching Simone with her peripheral vision. Simone made a false start at the chair with the booster seat, just to see Bernadette lunge for it. This was enough to cause Bernadette to hover near the chair, ignoring nature's call. (After all, you can't concentrate on going to the potty unless you're sure your seat is safe.)

After lunch the girls decided they wanted to watch *Beauty and the Beast*. The couch in front of the TV had only one blanket, which Simone grabbed.

> "I want that blanket!" hollered Bernadette, bursting into tears.

This time it was Simone who wore the smug smile.

> "Can you share the blanket?" I asked foolishly.

The reply was unanimously negative. Although she is the smaller of my two girls, Bernadette is quick to use physical force in pursuit of her goals. A tugging match ensued, complete with screaming, crying, and the occasional swinging of a free arm. Again, I settled the argument and brought in another blanket, so each could have her own.

The battle for territory and possession is not limited to inanimate objects. Often I have walked into the kitchen to see Kathy fixing dinner with a girl attached to each leg, like a tree with two competing vines trying to snake their way up to her shoulders. I know that if I can get one away, the other will follow, thus sacrificing myself so that all may eventually eat.

As I grab one, the other begins a whine that continues with increasing intensity until both are in my arms. Then Simone, in a gesture of affection, kisses my cheek. Bernadette does the same. Simone wraps her arms around my head to prevent her sibling from any further kissing. Bernadette grabs my hair and attempts to break the hold of Simone's locked arms. Feet begin to kick. I think to myself, "It's nice to be so popular."

Next comes bath time. This is always a time of chivalry.

"Who wants her hair washed first?" I ask.

"Bernadette," says Simone.

"Simone," says Bernadette.

"We'll flip a coin," I respond, putting this sensitive decision in the hands of fate.

The coin is tossed and the washing starts, each wailing in turn for her mother, who they apparently believe will save them from this torture.

After their baths are complete, we read and say prayers, and I tuck the girls in their beds.

"Daddy, why did you tuck Bernadette in first?"

"I take turns, remember, Simone? Last night you were first."

"But you always tuck her in first."

"No, we take turns."

"I was first tonight, Simone," announced Bernadette from her dark corner, happy to have one last triumph before calling it a day.

I stand in the doorway, savoring the moment. Life sure goes fast.

"Good night, girls. I love you both."

The Joys of Justice

I have discovered a sure-fire way to make Simone happy: punish her little sister.

It's foolproof. Nothing seems to put that special sparkle in Simone's eye, that look of delight on her face, better than a reprimand or punishment for Bernadette. An invitation for a trip to the ice-cream store may be met with a nonchalant "Okay." A suggestion that we play with toys evokes a luke-warm response. A walk down the street, a ride in the car, even a trip to the movies pales in comparison to the excitement of watching justice administered to Bernadette. It seems to warm Simone to the very core.

The standard punishment in our house is a "time-out." It's a modern-day version of my parent's tried and true practice of sending us to our rooms, except that a time-out is usually accomplished in a chair, on a couch, or in some other convenient sitting spot.

This makes time-outs much more suitable for parents of my generation, who tend to travel more than earlier generations and who have come to realize that bedrooms are not portable, making it difficult to mete out justice when away from home. In our age of jet flight, instant lottery tickets, and microwave ovens, it just doesn't seem appropriate to tell a child, "When we get home, you're confined to your room."

Simone, of course, has had many time-outs in her three-and-a-half years, but Bernadette has only recently come of age. In the early months of childhood babies just don't do anything that warrants punishment. When they do start to misbehave, children are able to maintain the myth that they don't understand the concepts of right, wrong, and punishment. No father could, in good conscience, punish a tiny child who had no idea she was doing anything wrong and who made no connection between her father's unexplained anger and her innocent and understandable desire to flush his wallet down the toilet.

Even grown men eventually learn that these little people are fully capable of knowing right from wrong and understanding the concept of discipline. So the time-outs begin. No self-respecting baby daughter would take the establishment of such precedents lying down, and Bernadette is no exception. Long before I decided that she was old enough to be punished, she mastered the art of emotional manipulation—a talent that will undoubtedly stand her in good stead in the years to come.

When she's happy, her smile warms the soul. When she's unhappy, her tears and facial expressions are guaranteed to make the disciplinarian feel like one of the lowest forms of life ever to inhabit the face of the earth.

The outbursts are an added bonus for an older sister. For Simone, the spectacle of seeing her younger sister punished is no short-lived sensation of quick gratification. No, this is an event that involves slowly building tensions, warnings, and reprimands of increasing severity that climax into an actual time-out with full fanfare. To observe this progression of events without being in trouble yourself is an experience to be savored and relished.

Here's an example: I entered my bedroom today to find Bernadette bent face down in my closet, flinging my shoes out into the middle of the floor.

> "Stop that," I insisted, "and please put all those shoes back."

Bernadette returned the shoes to their rightful place, one by one. Simone disclosed, quite self-righteously, that she hadn't touched my shoes.

Ten minutes later Bernadette was chewing on a pen and greeted me with a big blue smile.

> "Give me that pen," I said, "and stop taking things off my dresser. That's naughty."

After a brief interlude, Bernadette was observed dipping one of my best ties into the cat's water dish.

> "Bernadette, that's very naughty. Now give me that tie."

"No," she replied, a defiant look on her face.

We began a battle of wills in which I, the 185-pound adult, eventually triumphed over the 20-pound toddler. My tie, however, lost and went into the trash can. Bernadette went to her room for a time-out.

> "What are you doing with Bernadette?" Simone
> asked, beaming.
>
> "I'm giving her a time-out," I replied, only to see
> an added sparkle in Simone's eyes.

Simone searched the room to find one of Bernadette's favorite toys, which she began to play with in full view of her sister. Naturally, my sense of fairness cannot tolerate such provocation, so Simone was banished to another room without the toy. She positioned herself in a hallway so that she could visually monitor and enjoy Bernadette's predicament.

> "Bernadette got off her chair, Daddy."

Simone, with her deep sense of duty, had assumed the role of warden and stool pigeon.

> "*You* stay away from her, and if I catch you both-
> ering her again, *you'll* have a time-out too."

Simone trudged off down the hallway. Everything was ruined. She couldn't taunt her sister, couldn't watch her being punished, couldn't openly revel in her predicament. And to make things worse, now there was nobody to play with.

> "It's time to get Bernadette, Daddy. She's been in there long enough."

Simone's face was sympathetic, her voice soft and subdued. The excitement ran high when I released Bernadette. The two of them hugged, hopped around a little, then ran off holding hands. I smiled to myself as I watched them run down the hallway to the kitchen, sounds of laughter and glee filling the air.

Then I heard a cupboard open up and recognized the distinct sound of Tupperware in flight.

This Is Not Happy Fun Time

I caught my two girls playing in the road today, naked. They'd been, shall we say, high-spirited all day, and in an act of desperation Kathy had banished them from her sight. The last straw had been when they appeared in the kitchen with their clothes soaking wet. Kathy interrogated:

> "Why are your clothes all wet, girls?"
>
> "We poured the water on our heads."
>
> "What water?"
>
> "The water in our cups."
>
> "What cups?"
>
> "The cups in our room."
>
> "Did anything else get wet?"
>
> "Just our rug and Bernadette's pillow."

It had been that kind of day. They had been running, squealing, hollering, crying, laughing, jumping, slamming, singing, banging, climbing, bouncing, spraying, spilling, splattering, and singing since dawn.

It was now 5 P.M., and Kathy just wanted them to stay out of her sight for a while, so they were banished to an unspecified location—anywhere she couldn't see them. So they did the only logical thing: they ripped off their wet clothes and went outside to play.

I was relaxing after a full day of chores, and I heard their little voices, filled with joy and laughter, floating in the window. After a few minutes, I stood to peek into their world of play and saw them hopping like bunnies at the edge of the road, flinging dirt and leaves into the air. I called them to the front porch in my sternest, strictest, most authoritarian voice. They ran to me, engulfed in gleeful laughter.

"Look at us, Daddy. We're all muddy!"

Their hands and feet were black. Dirt was smeared over Bernadette's face, and both had taken pains to cover their bellies and legs with fresh mud.

"Look at our heinies," they beamed proudly, nearly dropping to the ground in laughter. "They're all muddy too!"

I began to scold them for being in the road, which is strictly forbidden in our family. They found this quite hilarious. Then their mother appeared in the doorway.

"Hose them down. They're filthy."

The orders sounded like they came from Cruella DeVille. I felt sorry for them—the water coming from the hose was cold. They acted as if I were running them through a tickling machine, giggling and snorting, while they shivered under the icy flow.

At the dinner table I tried to impress upon them the seriousness of their transgression.

> "I'm very angry," I explained. "The road is very
> dangerous, and you know you're not supposed
> to go in it. You could have been hurt by a car.
> I'm going to have to punish you."

They glanced at each other with held-back grins.

> "Oh, we're sorry, Daddy. We won't do it again."

They were nearly breaking out in guffaws. Even Kathy was trying to hide a smile. My next announcement got their attention.

> "There will be no books tonight and no television
> tomorrow. And if you misbehave any more, you'll
> be grounded to your room. And no more laugh-
> ing; this is not happy fun time."

Their smiles disappeared. My heart dropped.

Despite the fact that I knew they had done wrong, I felt like a heel. There was joy and happiness in the room, and I had extinguished it. I needed to make a serious point, and I succeeded, but at what price? Not a very high one, it turned out. They were soon laughing and giggling again.

"We can't watch TV, can we Daddy?"

The question was asked with a large smile.

"No books tonight!" they said cheerily, exchanging
glances and barely holding back their laughter.

They left the dinner table to run up and down the hallway,
filled with joy and devoid of remorse.

Or so I thought. After their baths, Simone came to me in
the kitchen.

"Daddy, I'm sorry I went in the road. I won't do
it again."

Her face was solemn, her voice sincere. She hugged me and
left the room without asking for a repeal of her punishment.
Immediately after that Bernadette came in and did the same
thing. It was clear that they both understood the gravity of
playing in the road and were genuinely sorry. They just
didn't want it to spoil their entire day. The happiness in
their lives and the pleasure of each other's company over-
powered all the anger I could muster.

If they deal with the world this way, I'll feel like a successful father.

Through a Child's Eyes

"It's Only a Movie"

The picture was something like this: David was holding one of those plastic golf clubs in his hands, the kind that doesn't really look like a golf club, but parents of young kids buy them anyway. This one had a white shaft, a bright orange handle, and a hollow, oversized head.

He was standing in the corner of the family room, next to a six-foot-tall fica—a favorite house plant of ours—shaped by summers outside. He took a back swing and made solid contact with the plant several times. This was a deliberate action; there was no golf ball in sight.

This kind of child's play presents an opportunity for parents to exercise either their most understanding and insightful parental response or simply yell, "Stop that!"

> "Don't worry, Mom," he said to Cheryl in a calm, reassuring voice before she had a chance to scold him. "This isn't happening. It's only a movie."

On one level, this little episode of early childhood behavior is fairly easy to understand. The child is deliberately doing something he knows he shouldn't do and watching how the parent reacts. For this situation, however, there is another possible explanation. Three months earlier we took him to his first movie in a real theater.

I vividly remember *my* first childhood trip to a movie theater. On a rainy Saturday in 1955 my mother took me to see *Bambi*. We were late, missing the first several minutes. I didn't realize until years later that, in all likelihood, our late arrival was a deliberate strategy to take care that I was not upset by the death of Bambi's mother in the opening scenes. My mother's hunch was right. I would have focused on that one part of the film and missed much of what followed in that hallmark child's film.

In a nearby town there was an old-time movie theater with a balcony and ushers who still wore uniforms. That's where we took David for his first movie. The theater is now divided, as are most old theaters, into Cinemas 1, 2, and 3. To me, it still looks like an old theater. We sat in what was once the balcony. A black plywood floor now extends from the balcony to the screen, creating an awkward second floor where one was never intended. An oversized antique chandelier still hangs from the ceiling, but it looks grotesquely out of proportion now that the floor is so close. There are virtually no lights, even when people arrive early, as we did, to "get good seats."

So this was the setting for his first movie. The film was *Home Alone,* the popular film about a young boy who is inadvertently left at home when his family leaves for a European vacation. In the course of the two-hour movie, the boy successfully defends himself against the repeated attempts of two thugs who try to enter his house. Pretty scary stuff for a four-year-old's first movie.

David's eyes were riveted to the large screen and the active visual images of this boy in a variety of funny and frightening scenes. The film was an upbeat, good-triumphs-over-evil sort, but nonetheless, there were scenes that obviously raised David's concern. (I thought of my mother's *Bambi* strategy.)

Kevin, the boy in *Home Alone,* sets traps that could only come from the mind of a small child. In one scene, Kevin places a black, gooey, tar-like substance on each of the cellar steps. As the intruder gains more confidence with each step up, he rather firmly steps on the business end of a nail, yells, and tumbles backward through all the black gook.

I looked to gauge David's reaction, then turned back to the screen. A steam iron was now tumbling down a laundry shoot and hitting the same character squarely on the forehead.

> "Don't worry, David," I said. "This is only a movie. These people are just pretending, and the man isn't really hurt."

So that was it. David didn't refer to my remark for months. Then, all of a sudden, as though it had been circling in his mind the whole time, out it came, delivered to his mom with the same calmness and reassurance that he had heard from me during the matinee in the old theater.

While I would like to believe that Cheryl and I are perfect parents, I know we make mistakes. We are the kind of parents, however, who talk about, think about, and worry about how we respond to David. All child development theory aside, a good portion of parenting unfortunately comes in the form of impulsive responses to child behavior. For that reason, the parent's mood and the circumstances of the moment often play critical roles in decisions of how to behave. In the situation of the golf swing and the house plant, the impulse to punish the little golfer would have been a mistake.

The only thing to do was laugh and hug this little boy with his plastic golf club, standing next to the bruised house plant. After all, he had just contributed to the family folk-lore. Little does he now understand how many times he will hear this story repeated in years to come.

Outsmarting Dad

Simone taught me a lesson last night: our VCR has magical healing properties.

I came down to the family room to retrieve her for dinner while she was watching one of her favorite movies, and I explained to her that we would stop the movie, eat dinner, and return for its conclusion. She agreed happily, and all was fine when I stopped the tape. As I picked her up, however, she was jolted by sharp abdominal pains.

Upstairs at the dinner table Simone wanted to eat but was repeatedly attacked by pains "inside my tummy." Her screams varied in pitch and intensity, clearly proving that these were not steady, dull aches, but pains that attacked without warning and with great severity. I was concerned.

> "No doctors," she said when she sensed my alarm. "Can I just lie down?"
>
> "Sure, Sweetheart," I responded, anxious to try anything that might ease her discomfort.
>
> "Can I lie on the couch and watch the rest of *Mermaid?*"

The expression on her little face was brave. Yet she was reaching out for sympathy, help, and support.

"Of course you can, Honey."

I carried her downstairs, prepared her special pillow, gently positioned her on the couch, and adjusted the angle of the television so that she wouldn't have to strain to watch her movie. She lay patiently, quietly, suffering bravely in silence.

"Can you stay with me, Daddy?"

"Of course I will," I said cheerily, gladly forfeiting the remainder of my dinner if it would help Simone feel better.

Just a few minutes after the tape resumed playing an amazing thing happened: somehow the rays from the television gently bathed Simone's stomach and healed the discomfort.

First she crawled across the couch to sit on my lap. Then she discovered that she could watch the movie by staring at the reflection in my glasses. She helped the Little Mermaid sing her parts. Most incredible, however, was what happened when Bernadette came down from dinner. Bernadette is not one to miss out on anything, including movies, but her attention span isn't compatible with feature-length films. About five minutes after arriving, she began to play with Simone's stuffed bear.

Throwing caution to the wind, Simone leaped from the couch to separate Bernadette from the toy. A battle ensued, and Simone held her own, despite her weakened and pained condition.

Then the dancing started.

> "Watch this, Daddy," she insisted, as she twirled with the grace of a ballerina, leaping and running around the room.

Bernadette joined in, urging me to watch her instead and raising the decibel level high enough to drown out the television.

I sat amazed. I wonder if doctors are aware of this radical method of treatment? Surely it deserves some study. Only twenty minutes ago I had been ready to take Simone to the emergency room, and now, through the magic of Walt Disney and the soothing screen, my daughter is well again. It's truly a miracle.

After I put Simone to bed, I pondered the situation. How did she learn to fool me like that? Not from my example; I wouldn't dare try to avoid household chores by faking sick. I'd be caught for sure. Certainly not from Kathy. Could one of her little friends have taught her? It seems unlikely.

No, I don't believe anyone taught her how to do that—
I think such talents are within us all. I admit that, on
occasion, as a child, I too had faked sickness. And come
to think of it, I don't remember being taught how either.
As our minds develop, we try different techniques to help
ease our journey through life, and we learn through trial
and error what works and what doesn't. Simone crossed
a threshold last night.

Fatherhood will never be boring.

Summer Wonders

To children, a summer is longer than a year. Innocence and wonder surround everything they do.

Playing outside after dinner is the best kind of playing. David, at age two, already senses the unfairness of going to bed before it is dark. Knowing the day is almost over, he tries to fit a lot into his after-dinner hour.

Tonight he sat on the curb studying the small pebbles and pools of dry sand collecting where the road folded up at the edge. He pointed to some grass that had found its way through a crack. Then, arms windmilling, he began practicing jumping from the curb to the road.

Next came an investigation of the storm sewer. First he peered through the steel straps into the pools of water that always seem to be there, even when the street is dry. Then the search started for small pebbles, stones anything he could find. One at a time, and with great care, he dropped them into the black water below.

An evening thunderstorm, should it occur, opens new choices for him. He goes straight to the puddles. Kids are fascinated with puddles, and David is no exception. He steps in slowly with one foot, then steps in again with more confidence and both feet. Next he rides through it in his fire engine, forward, backward, and forward again, always with his head twisted around to see the ripples made by the wheels.

On some nights, David heads directly for the woods. (How easily I remember growing up near a wooded section and sensing the possibility for exploration that woods offer. Streams, salamanders, worms, branches, trails, skunk cabbage, bugs. Everything feels different and special when you step into the woods. There are wonderful smells and sounds that cannot be found in a suburban neighborhood.)

On other nights David moves sand in the sandbox. Into the bucket, out of the bucket and out of the box. His imagination gives each action a purpose.

We live in a neighborhood of about ten houses and lots of other kids. David would play all day with Julie, Carolyn, Laura, Kevin, Carla, and Maggie if the time were his to fill. Big kids ride bicycles and chew gum, but to him they seem to tire out too quickly.

Watching a child play presents parents and other adults with the chance to be children again and to be reminded of the ease and simplicity with which children learn. You don t need a degree in developmental psychology to figure this out.

When children see something new, they approach it, pick it up, and try to do all kinds of things with it. No fear, no

102

bias. Everything is approached the same way. To David, every new experience is an opportunity to *try something.*

There are many "not yets" in David's life. Aspects of summer that bother adults are "not yet" a bother to him. Playing outside in the hot noon sun, biting the end off a drippy ice-cream cone, picking up a wiggling, slimy worm, or hearing the buzz of a mosquito are just part of his day.

In time he will observe that some people do not like thunderstorms, mosquitoes, or melting ice cream. Knowingly and unknowingly, we give to our children our own attitudes. He will learn to complain about humidity, rain, and bug bites. This summer was his first to explore—and his first to remember.

Spending these summer evenings with David brings reminders of what it feels like to be a child. The feelings come back with startling ease, suggesting that they never really left. My own life was shaped by a childhood filled with summers like these. The difference is, when you are older, summers last about a minute.

Restless Nights

Last night, after being called into my son's room for the fourth time, I had one of those "who's in charge here" dilemmas. The first time he was snoring and having difficulty breathing through his nose. Next his blankets were off, and after that he had to go to the bathroom. He had a stuffy nose, it was twenty degrees outside, and his room was cold. He was thirsty and was in the middle of his third night sans diaper.

Any one of these events is an understandable cause for unrest. Taken as a group, they were clearly reason enough for David's not wanting to sleep alone. Sleep, to a parent of a young child, is a precious thing. "Sleep together" does not really mean sleep together. It means Mommy or Daddy stays awake while David goes back to sleep. I am fully aware of the hard-line alternative approach here: just stop going into a child's bedroom, and eventually the child will realize that being alone is not such a terrible thing.

I remember my own childhood sleepless nights and the technique I used. I would call for my mother, first very softly, and then each time slightly louder. I would repeat it perhaps a dozen times, pausing between each call to listen for the familiar sounds of someone getting out of bed and walking down the hall toward me.

Last month my wife and I attended a seminar on common

behaviors of four-year-olds given by a child psychologist. She gave us some pretty accurate—and pretty frightening— pictures of what to expect from David. Somehow, the seminar shifted to our favorite topic of late: sleep (or lack of it). After she told us about common bedtime behaviors, she also asked one parent—whose child wakes frequently and cannot get back to sleep—the following question.

"Does he have an active mind?"

That was a startling question. How many nights in my adult life have I awakened and found myself incapable of getting back to sleep because of the meaningless anxieties that stalk me at three in the morning? The "active mind." I am not talking here about serious issues—life's major decisions. I am talking about staying awake because of the screen-door latch I have to buy at the hardware store or the decision of which ground cover to plant in a shady corner of the yard.

So there I was, sitting on the edge of David's bed in the wee hours of the morning. The teddy bear night light shone dimly on one wall, and the sounds of an early winter night wind could be heard outside the north window. Why, I pondered, were this four-year-old's eyes open, despite his very obvious search for a comfortable position? Where was David's "active mind" taking him?

What child doesn't have an active mind when you consider

the bombardment of new experiences each day brings? Children learn from observation, trial, and error. Adults often misunderstand the nature and intensity of play as a learning experience. When he wakes up during the night, he thinks about the day.

During the previous day we had watched together, for the first time, an award-winning video entitled *The Snowman.* Based on the book by Raymond Briggs, the story centers on the magic that develops between a young boy, a snow storm, and a man the boy makes from snow. David rolled over on his back, reacting for the first time to this video during my fourth visit to his room that night.

"Daddy, why doesn't my snowman walk?"

Now this is an interesting dilemma. If I give him a curt, unresponsive answer, I do not honor the sincerity of his need. He wants an answer, and he will remember it. If I launch into a major discussion about the difference between dreams and reality, between the snowman in the video and the snowman in his yard, we may be up for hours. I am fearful. However, I opt for the long version and discover once again that I cannot predict the behavior of a child. He simply says, "Oh," and goes to sleep. I returned to my bed thinking of my childhood snowmen. The active mind. Why do rest and inspiration both come from darkness?

Fast Forward

David operates four remote control devices, three phone keypads, a calculator, a computer keyboard, and two garage door openers. This is not unusual for a child in today's world, even at age three.

With so much written about rapidly changing technology and its effects on the human condition these days, the topic has become tiresome. Life occurs in cycles, of course, and today's changes in technology have caused some to worry about the future of our civilization. I am not worried at all.

People who lived from the late 1800s through the early 1900s—my great-grandparents—survived far more rapid changes. In a relatively short time span, society was given the first radio transmissions, automobile transportation, air flight, x-rays, and electric lights. The discovery of the electron, the cure for malaria, $E=MC^2$, and myriad other changes occurred at a staggering pace.

Even those who are reluctant to embrace new technology eventually accept it in one form or another. For some it may be a microwave oven, a touch-tone phone, or a sophisticated security system. I have simple tastes, and my technology of choice is the video camera. I still marvel at the high-quality, immediate visual images I can capture. Whether the shot is of a child's bike ride, deer wandering through the yard, or the first flowers of spring, I pop in the cassette and shoot.

In my family, this falls in with a picture-taking tradition. My father bought an 8mm movie camera when I was a child—frontier technology for the time. We spent many an Easter Sunday walking Grandma around the front yard before church, as though this were something we would do if we did not have the camera. And who does not remember a family gathering around an early home projector? Rarely did this go well. Even if we were successful at threading the film through the sprockets and into the take-up reel, the bulb would likely burn out before the two-minute film ended. The surprise comes with the realization that, despite those annoyances, we kept right on filming and projecting family images for years.

So now I watch videos, and I watch David as he pushes the rewind button to view a scene over and over again. We learn by repetition. Put a remote control rewind button in a child's hands and watch what he chooses to learn. For my son, it's a variety of images. He is fascinated with early scenes of him crying as he was being given a bath, and he always asks why we let him cry. His particular favorite is the tape of a local Labor Day parade, a procession I have now seen well over a hundred times.

Visual experiences are powerful links to memory. I can recall television episodes from my own early childhood—and

I only saw the shows once. In those days, when a show was a rerun, people didn't watch a second time. For a young child, learning starts with repetition. We tape David's favorite children's television shows, and he watches each one at least a dozen times over the span of a few months. Imagine the potential impact of this on how he learns. He can control the technology, pushing it forward or backward and choosing the images until he learns all he wants.

Grandparents marvel at a child's video skills. They grew up in a world without computers or videotapes. For some elders these are futuristic gadgets, superfluous things that advertisers have convinced us we need. Others simply fear change.

There is no question that technological advances are ahead of our ability to grasp them. Comedians now do routines about the flashing 12:00 on most VCRs. Today, computers interact with video, laser, and other media in a way that is foreign to most people. Schools have multimedia encyclopedias. When you look up John Fitzgerald Kennedy, you not only get the typical encyclopedia stuff, but you can view him debate Nixon, deliver his inaugural address, and drive by a Dallas book depository—all by poking a computer keyboard.

Technology is new only to those who lived before its arrival. To a young child, none of this is new. Today's children never knew life before the microchip, just as I never knew life before the picture tube. Each generation has its own fast forward.

Questions, Questions, Questions

Question 1

"What sound does a giraffe make?" David asked
one morning at breakfast.

This was something I had never pondered before and now
found myself struggling to answer.

Having a child changes you. I am just now beginning to
understand the truth of that statement. Before David was
born, I was a school principal and talked daily with parents
about family problems. Often, when I discussed a child's
behavior or situation with a doubting parent and offered
my suggestions, the parent would look at me and ask, "Are
you a parent?"

I was thirty-three then; I thought I had all the answers, and
I always recoiled at this question. At the time I did not draw
any meaning from the fact that so many parents asked me
the same question.

Answers like "None of your business," or "Your child's
behavior and how you act have nothing to do with whether
or not I have a child" remained unexpressed. Instead, I
usually said, "Not yet." Parents listened politely and then
dismissed in some measure whatever I said next.

To be an educator is to ask and answer questions with direction, purpose, and compassion. I make a living by answering questions, but none are more challenging than those asked by a young child.

Through language a child expresses thought. Questions are the means children use to form thoughts about the unknown and to confirm the known. To a parent, questions asked by a young child are revealing because they are the first demonstration of thought. They offer a fascinating look at how children derive meaning from their environments.

Questions 2, 3, 4, and 5

Children think all the time. Their early years consist of exploration, trial and error, and reflection about what they see, do, and hear. Every experience is an opportunity to learn, and, as a result, questions come naturally and rapidly.

"Can I see my eyebrow?"

"Do I like mustard?"

"Is Mommy in that speaker?"

"Are you old?"

Adults' answers to questions are a surprising source of influence and, at times, unwanted authority in a child's life. Through the dialogue that comes with this process is a responsibility to listen carefully, be patient, and give full attention to a child's perspective, even when the parent really doesn't want to answer any more questions. Shut off a child with abruptness or disinterest and you shut off the child's thought process, his opportunity to learn.

Question 6

In our house the questions often come at mealtimes. Routines are important to our sense of family, so we talk together when we eat. At age three, during a bad-mood episode one morning, David threw a bowl of cereal up in the air.

> After I had talked to him about how babies—not big boys—throw cereal when they are mad, he asked, "Daddy, what do big boys throw when they are mad?"

We have decided not to make the kitchen table a war zone where parents battle children over what will and will not be eaten. This is not always easy to do. Especially when we are trying to get David to drink something he hates: milk.

We don't give in, however; we try a variety of strategies ranging from de facto statements to not-so-skillful negotiations, laced with promises of good things to come if he just takes three more swallows.

I am surprised at how easy it is to say the wrong thing to a child. Phrases such as "because I said so" or "just do it" seem always ready to roll off my tongue. Parents find themselves saying things to their children that were said to *them* a generation ago, often with equally poor results. So there I was, actually saying, "If you drink your milk, it will make you grow bigger." Astoundingly, this worked.

Question 7

Later that night, during his "bedtime stories"—when we usually talk about the day's events instead of reading—David observed:

> "Daddy, apple juice doesn't make you bigger. Just milk."

> After a silent pause, when he obviously was thinking very seriously, he asked, "Am I bigger now?"

Question 8

Grandma and Grandpa were looking at houses in town with a local Realtor.

> "They might buy a house," David's mom explained when he asked where they had gone.

This clearly puzzled him.

> "Will they carry it home?" he asked, as he
> thought further about this pursuit.

Question 9

We have a dog, an adolescent golden retriever, named
Cassie, who bowls over house guests. But she lets David
jump on her, pull her lip, and poke her ears and face. She
not only tolerates these activities, but seems to welcome
them in quiet ecstasy. David often watches Cassie's behavior silently.

> Once, when he asked if Cassie had to go out-
> side, he said, "Cassie goes to the bathroom out-
> side, but I don't go outside because I don't have
> a tail, right?"

What triggers a child's question? For David, there are many
sources. Sometimes he asks a question when he sees
something unusual; sometimes when he hears a story or a
song; and other times when he remembers an incident that
happened months ago and has never talked about. It's as
though the thought had been trapped inside him, unable to
get out until now.

Then there are the questions he asks when he knows the
answer and wants confirmation, or when he knows the
answer and wants a different answer. Aunt Edith died last

spring. Aside from knowing that my mother died before he was born, this was his first experience with death. With precision and care he asks the same questions, in the same order each time, while knowing all the time what each answer will be.

Cheryl and I are the kind of parents who read books about parenting, who watch other parents, and who talk about parent-child relations with others. We know the ways we act as parents that we want to change.

We know that we indulge David too much by agreeing to his requests to carry him at times. Trying to reverse a pattern like this is not easy. It requires incredible persistence, and even then there are unintended consequences as he thinks through an obvious change in practice.

Cheryl took him to a farm with a group of mothers and other three-year-olds—none of whom were carried around by moms—so it gave her a good opportunity to use comparative logic, something that rarely works. But it did that day, and he walked around the whole time with other kids, not once asking to be carried. Later that day, after returning home, he asked to be carried again and announced, "I only have to walk at farms."

His reactions to such situations are not that difficult to figure out. David is applying logic; he is attempting to make sense out of the world he experiences as a three-year-old. If you let it happen, talking and playing with a young child will change you. Despite the appearance of play and fluff, the daily activity of children is a mixture of exploration, thought, and analysis. Quite simply, it is hard work. See it as something less, and you miss the importance of childhood learning.

Youthful spontaneity and wonder challenge parents who allow themselves to enter into a child's world. Moments of childhood innocence are both exhilarating and frightening. Exhilarating because through children we get a second chance at life, a chance to be free of the burdens we place on ourselves as adults and to see life as one big opportunity. And there's the fear, too—the fear of change. The appearance of simplicity in a child's life compels adults to redefine their own lives.

Question 10

The other morning while lying in bed, David yelled, "Daddy, do you know where you are?"

First Falls

Parents know that life is unpredictable. Just when you think you understand what is happening now and presume what will happen next, a child will say something that paints a different picture.

Like many young children, David has had his share of ear infections. They are the reason for most of his trips to the doctor. He hates ear exams. The doctor sticks that shiny metal thing in his ear and pumps a little ball, injecting air into his ear to see if the eardrum moves. David has more fear about this than anything else.

At age three, David had his first stitches. Lots of parents have this experience. The child gets cut. The wound is visible. It bleeds unendingly. The child is scared, and so is the parent. In those quick moments of crisis, the mind runs through all sorts of possibilities. First: the big picture. *He'll live.* Second: action. *To the doctor or the emergency room?* Third: fear. *Will there be a scar?*

Like most bumps, cuts, and bruises, this one happened at a time when David was happily playing, unaware of the events about to unfold. Suddenly the dog moves one way. He moves the other. They collide. He flies face first, and his forehead strikes the edge of the coffee table. We have a cut. We have blood. We have screams. The dog stands still, puzzled, toy still clenched in her teeth.

We opted quickly for the doctor's office. The cut was close to the eye, which was now swollen shut. The nurse recognized that this was not a routine visit and led us directly into an examining room. The entire time Cheryl and I reassured David that he would be all right and that the doctor would make him feel better. He looked skeptical.

Medicine is a curious business. To feel better, sometimes you have to endure more pain. This is impossible to explain rationally to a child whose eye is puffed shut. You know what happened next: the pain worsened.

First came the cotton swab soaked in cold, clear liquid. This produced a stinging sensation, directly into the cut, which—then free of blood—was deeper than I wanted to see. After giving David hollow assurances, like, "We have to clean the cut, so you will feel better," and the biggest lie of all, "She is almost done," I knew my credibility was low.

When the cotton swab disappeared, the ice pack arrived. Everyone knows that ice keeps swelling down, so this made considerable sense, except to the child with the wound. The ice hurt.

The cut required stitches. We knew it. The nurse knew it, and the doctor knew it. David didn't. If you are a cautious parent, you are, at this point, wondering how much detail to offer.

"A stitch is like sewing with thread. It will help the cut heal." And so forth. But David knew that sewing required a needle, the one detail I avoided.

Let's be honest here, Novocain also hurts.

Two adults should be able to hold a three-year-old in a stationary position, having the obvious size and weight advantage. Since David's cut was close to his eye, moving his head—even slightly—during the process would be dangerous. So we had to hold him absolutely still while the doctor probed the open cut from four angles with the Novocain.

David was on his back with his head turned so that his left cheek was flat against the table. The nurse held his head firmly. I stood near his knees, leaning on them with my chest while holding both his arms in my hands.

There were few moments when I felt so needed and helpless at the same time. I stayed with him though it all, stroking him, acknowledging that this was not fun, and trying feebly to convince him that the torture was almost over. But I could not control his pain.

So there he was on the examining table, having endured the pain of the actual fall, the cotton swab, the ice pack, the Novocain, and all of these new experiences in rapid succession. He had a white sheet over his head to protect his eyes from the bright examining light. I was standing, bent over at his side, sticking my head under a corner of the sheet so I could see him. I could see that, between sobs, he was thinking about something.

"Daddy," he whispered, "are they going to check my ears, too?"

Time with Dad

Stories

No one ever told me that my duties as a father would include storytelling, but it has emerged as an important element in my job description.

It started innocently enough, with my wife telling our two daughters about how their uncle Tommy was hit by a car when he was four years old—part of her effort to stress the importance of never going into the road by themselves.

Then one day, when my oldest daughter fell and skinned her knee, I told her about how I had done the same when I was little. Before long, childhood stories became standard fare at any event in our household, no matter how small.

On the eve of a trip, we tell about similar trips we took as children. First day of school. ("Sure, I remember it.") Younger sister always gets put to bed first. ("Let me tell you what happened to *me* at bedtime when I was little.") Grandma coming to visit. ("I remember when my grandma came to stay for a while.")

These stories give our children a sense of history while conveying important lessons about life. They also have created a hunger for information that cannot be satiated. It is nearly impossible to keep up with the request for new stories. I have come to fear the inevitable second question:

"Daddy, will you tell me a story?"

"Sure, which one would you like?"

"How about one I've never heard before."

Unfortunately, I have only thirty-four years' worth of stories to tell, and I feel obligated to screen out all those that include activities I wouldn't like my own daughters to emulate—a severe limitation in my case.

"How about the time I hit the home run?"

"Already heard that."

"The Boy Scouts contest when I won the green pup tent?"

"You've told that before."

"The story of Pepper, our dog who was run over
   by a car?"

"We know that by heart."

"The time Ruthie cracked her chin open?"

"No."

"The day I fell off the slide?"

That was old news too.

In addition to having a voracious appetite for new stories,
my daughters have set strict standards for their contents.
They must include moments of drama, as well as a clear
beginning and end. Preferably they should have some type
of moral. Since the girls automatically assume that all of
the stories are true, I insist that they be real-life episodes
that are told as accurately as possible.

Also, the stories must stand up to questioning about the
most intricate details.

"One time, when I was a little boy, Grandma Joan
   and Pop-Pop took us to Cape Cod."

"Was Ruthie a little girl?" interrupted Simone.

"Yes, Ruthie was a little girl. So, Grandma Joan
   and Pop-Pop took us to Cape Cod to stay at a
   beautiful hotel called the Colony Beach."

"Did you jump on the beds?"

"Yes, we jumped on the beds. So, we stayed at this wonderful hotel, which had small kitchens in the rooms, a nice pool, and a beautiful beach."

"Did Grandma Joan cook in the kitchen?"

"Yes."

"What kind of food?"

"Hot dogs and pasta and hamburgers. So, anyway, one night, while we were staying at the hotel, Grandma Joan and Pop-Pop were invited to a party. They checked with the people who owned the hotel, and they had a nice daughter who was just the right age to baby-sit us."

"What was her name?"

Heaven forbid that I might have forgotten it.

And so the storytelling continues, punctuated by questions. Even a minor story is stretched into a greatly exaggerated tale through this process. Most amazing is the girls' ability to memorize the details, then use the information to correct and question us later.

"You jumped on the beds at that hotel, didn't you? And you had hot dogs and pasta and hamburgers for food?"

They love these stories so much. I think back to the days when my own parents told me stories about *their* childhoods—stories that remain with me to this day. In fact, I remember accounts of my grandparents' childhoods. Stories keep memories alive, keep pictures sharp in our minds. They help us relive the moments of our own lives and allow our children to share in those moments.

I guess what touches me the most is the fact that I used to ask my parents to tell me stories, but for some reason I stopped one day, and I've never asked them since. I don't remember the last time I asked, and I don't remember why I stopped asking. I may have become preoccupied with baseball or television or books or friends, or any old thing. The fact is that one day I just stopped asking for stories. Some day my daughters will stop too.

I hope they ask me to tell them a story tonight.

Saturday

A young child's Saturdays are filled with routines as predictable as many adults' work schedules. Parents see the day as a balance between time with a child and time spent cleaning the house, paying the bills, working in the yard, and dozens of other tasks that clutter weekend to-do lists. Children, however, have a different perspective on the day.

Child development experts claim that time is an abstract concept, one that young children struggle to grasp. Not so in my house. To David, Saturday is time to be spent with Daddy. Period. Actually, our Saturdays have entered a pattern of activity that neither of us will surrender easily. It starts sometime on Thursday, when David realizes that tomorrow is Friday and then comes "Saturday-Sunday," the pair of days considered as one.

For adults who have young children, Saturday morning starts at sunrise, or before. In one way or another, kids figure out quickly that Mom and Dad prefer to spend far too much time in bed, and they develop a repertoire of behaviors to signal the end of a night's sleep. A call, footsteps, the banging of drumsticks, or simply "Can I have breakfast now?" starts the day.

Once up, we make a big deal of Saturday breakfast. We either cook something special or go to our favorite local spot, which serves Mickey Mouse pancakes—three cakes as a head with two ears, topped with whipped cream and chocolate chips to complete the resemblance. The owners walk from table to table, talking the way people talk to friends. It is likely to be one of the few times during the day when the three of us are together.

Families with small children, full-time moms, and working dads are uncommon today. Demographers claim that these Ozzie-and-Harriet situations, which included seven out of ten United States households in the 1950s, now describe only seven out of every one hundred. Those of us who are able to choose that family style in the 1990s are clearly a minority. However, even recognizing the risk of gender stereotyping that can victimize women who stay home with their children, moms see Saturdays as their time alone, time when Dad has the kids.

If there is ever a remake of "Ozzie and Harriet," my town would make a great setting. After all, a town that has had a hundred-foot flagpole in its main intersection for nearly a century has a certain respect for tradition. On Saturdays, car after car of dads and kids pass that flagpole en route to soccer games, community activities, and other destinations.

David and I go to four or five stores—the same stores—every Saturday morning. For us, the first stop is always the "cleaning man," David's favorite. This is not surprising given that, without fail, Tony has lollipops for kids—one of the best indicators that the late B. F. Skinner might have been right after all. Maybe if Skinner had used lollipops instead of food pellets, he would have taught pigeons to do more than play Ping-Pong.

Because this is a time of environmental consciousness, the recycling center is our next stop. Cars line up with tin, plastic, glass, newspaper, and so forth. So many cars, in fact, now go to the landfill that politicians and service club reps work the lines to pass out leaflets. No one comments on the irony of giving people more paper to take home with them after they have just spent all this time gathering junk mail and newspapers into neatly tied bundles.

Next comes the bank (ours is still open every Saturday) and the post office, then the hardware store—lots of dads here. If management experts want more examples of customer-oriented businesses, they should come to this hardware store. The owners greet you by name, talk about the weather and the schools—and always have the one thing I need.

By this time David is usually ready to go home and tell Mom about each stop on the morning route, starting with what color lollipop Tony gave him and ending with the list of people we saw in the hardware store.

Depending on the season, Saturday afternoon is altogether different from Saturday morning. Generally the two per-spectives are something like this: David thinks of the after-noon as time spent exclusively with Dad, playing inside and outside. I try to sneak in a quick project, football game, or nap, but am regularly unsuccessful at this. Quite simply, Saturday is his day.

One has to learn to be a good parent. Parenting expertise is not something we are born with. Nor do we read about it or observe it—until we need it. I have learned to be less selfish and more willing to give myself to someone else. This is not easy for a baby boomer, a card-carrying member of the "me generation." If David wants to throw a Frisbee, cut some paper, or build a tower, he wants me doing it too. And while I know that it is important for him to learn to play alone, I always join him when he asks.

How much longer will he be interested in Dad on Saturdays? I don't know the answer, and I am not sure I want to know. When the day comes that Saturdays are mine again, I know I will long for the days when they were not.

Reviving White Lightning

I set out this morning with one goal: to revive an old white Peugeot that was abandoned in my backyard two years ago. My plan was to get "White Lightning" running long enough to drive it to the junkyard. For a nonmechanic with two left thumbs, it was an ambitious goal. What's more, I had help.

I began in solitude, which I enjoyed for about half an hour. This allowed me time to skin the first layer off my knuckles and swear profusely without any "little ears" around to hear my example and repeat the colorful phrases in church and around town.

Kathy then came out with Simone and Bernadette.

> "I'll take the kids with me," she offered, eliciting an immediate response from Simone.
>
> "I have to stay here and help Daddy," she said emphatically.

Simone gets very adamant about such things, but I do enjoy her company. So I said she could stay.

I explained to her that I was fixing the car and would be very busy. She understood completely. I picked up a tool and went back under the hood.

"Can I help you, Daddy?"

"Sure."

"Can I use this one?" she asked, picking a crescent wrench out of my toolbox.

"Sure," I replied.

"What do you want me to fix?"

A reasonable question.

"How about the grill," I suggested, pointing to that area of the car.

"No, I think I'd better fix this instead," she explained as she started to bang on the bumper with the wrench.

She repeated this routine with my needle-nose pliers, hammer, screwdriver, and electrical tape. Soon it was time for lunch.

We had a wonderful lunch of cheese sandwiches and juice and watched one of her Disney videos while eating. Then it was back to work.

Soon after we recommenced, Kathy arrived home with Bernadette. My head was deep under the hood, my hands and forearms covered with grease, and my attention focused on the task at hand. I guess Kathy figured I needed another helping hand, so she left Bernadette with me.

"What's this?" Bernadette's little voice asked.

"Huh?"

"What's this, Daddy?"

"That's the box that holds my drill bits," I
 answered.

"Can I open it?"

"Sure."

That is not the proper response, unless you want to spend
ten minutes on your hands and knees looking through the
grass for drill bits.

After I had reboxed my drill bits and gotten back under the
hood, Bernadette wanted to help again.

"Here, Daddy, have this," she said as she dropped
 one of my medium-sized wrenches into the
 engine compartment.

I heard the sickening sound of a tool wedging itself into a
tiny, hard-to-reach place in the machinery. As I tried to
retrieve it, I heard her sweet little voice again.

"Here, Daddy. Have this."

Again the sound of metal falling against metal.

> "Please, Bernadette, don't give me any
> more tools."
> "Okay."

I contorted my arm and shoulder to retrieve the first tool,
climbed under the car for the second, and returned them
both to my box. Back to work. The two girls began a thor-
ough exploration of my toolbox.

> "What's this, Daddy?"
> "I don't know," I replied without looking.
> "Can I get it?"
> "Okay."
> "What's in here?"
> "Razor blades! Now put that down."

It was time for my two daughters to go help their mother.

With the help of my friend Nick, an aerospace engineer and
automobile genius, I finally got the car started, only to drive
it to the end of my driveway, where it died forever. My little
helpers and I were unsuccessful. I pushed the car back to a
location near the house.

Later, I had it towed to the junkyard.

The Best Father's Day Present

Children have a way of helping you focus on your own strengths and weaknesses. Here's an example.

I've been known to drive too fast on occasion. Simone and Bernadette have witnessed and commented on the results. Last week we were making the two-hour trip to visit Grandma Joan and Pop-Pop, and as usual we were behind schedule. The road was dark, and I was impatient. Simone became aware of the flashing lights at about the same time I did.

> "Daddy, what are those red lights?"
>
> "That's a police car, Simone."
>
> "Why are they blinking?"
>
> "Because the policeman would like me to pull over so he can talk to me."
>
> "Why does he want to talk to you, Daddy?"

At this point, Kathy chimed in.

> "Because Daddy's driving too fast!"
>
> "Is he going to give you another pink paper, Daddy?"

Then Bernadette woke up and started crying.

> "Shhh, Berna," said Simone helpfully. "This

policeman wants to talk to Daddy and give him a
pink paper because he's driving too fast."

The trooper was understanding and let me go with a warning, and we started off again into the black night.

"He's driving too fast!" exclaimed Bernadette's
small voice from the darkness behind me.

"He's driving too fast!" said the voice again, twenty
seconds later.

"He's driving too fast!" she said after another
twenty seconds.

"No, Bernadette, I'm driving slower now."

"He's driving too fast!" responded the voice.

I looked over at Kathy, who delighted in seeing justice dis-
pensed so effectively. My sentence was to hear my crime
repeated over and over again by my irrepressible daughter.
It seemed like an eternity.

Although children seem to notice and dwell upon the tini-
est parental mistake, their lasting impressions of parents
are often more positive. Their true impressions come out
when I get home from work and they come running to
greet me, or when they fall down and cry for a soothing
hug, or when I'm digging an old hunk of cement out of the
backyard to clear a space for their new swingset and
Simone observes:

"It's a good thing you're a strong, brave daddy to dig that out for our swingset. Isn't it, Daddy?"

To have my little girl look up to me as more than a dad—a hero, a builder, a savior—that's the best Father's Day present a guy could get. (Even if it wasn't Father's Day quite yet.) It comes spontaneously, from the heart. That's what makes it special.

Those words warmed me through and through, and they gave me a challenge to live up to, a high standard to aspire to over time. I'll never forget them.

I wonder if Simone will.

Setting the Record Straight

I have been informed by my chief editor, best friend, main cheerleader, and lifelong partner, Kathy, that one of the people in this book has been misrepresented. Considering her virtually unconditional support of my efforts to write, this comment came as a surprise.

> "When they read this, they'll think that all I feed the kids are hot dogs and beans, and all I do is yell at them," she lamented. "They'll think I'm a bad mother!"

That, dear reader, would be a terrible injustice, so I'd like to set the record straight.

With a new baby comes the necessity to make some tough choices. A woman can choose to stay home with her child, and, in the process, torpedo a career, slash the family income, and—in many cases—reduce her career potential for life. For all her sacrifices, she will receive little recognition, except for the occasional condemnations from people who say she is "wasting her education" or "selling out" the progress women have made in recent decades.

On the other hand, a woman can choose to work, virtually guaranteeing herself an endless string of daycare hassles, work pressures, and concerns about the effect of this choice on her family. In many cases, new moms shoulder

the work of raising the baby with no reduction of responsi-
bilities in other areas of life. Survey after survey tells us
that women with careers, working as many hours as their
husbands, still do more than their share of the work
around the house. Being a working mother, whether for
necessity or ambition, has undoubtedly caused many a
bright career to slow down, and caused many great moms
to become overworked and underappreciated.

Each choice has a price—and the price can be steep. Being
a mom in the '90s is complicated. Sometimes it seems as if
it's hard to come out ahead, no matter what you do.

When Simone was born, Kathy made the decision to give
up a budding career so she could stay home and be a full-
time mom to our new daughter. We both understood that
sacrifices would accompany the loss of nearly half our
income. Since then we have often eyed with envy the vaca-
tions, expensive cars, dinners out, and generally higher
lifestyle of the two-income families all around us.

We've had some tight times, particularly early on. There
were weeks when Kathy's had to get creative with our
meals to get us to the next paycheck. She's made do with
clothes several years old when her friends all had new
wardrobes. She's settled for weekend car trips with the kids
when others were jetting off to the islands for quick,
romantic getaways.

Has she ever complained? Yes. Has she ever gotten angry? Yes. Have we ever had disagreements—loud and not so loud—about how our limited financial resources would be used? Yes. Has Kathy ever wavered from her belief that our children would benefit from a full-time mom and her commitment to be there for them? No.

Along with the income, Kathy gave up a significant source of personal gratification. People like to talk about what they "do," meaning, of course, their occupations outside the home. Many make the assumption that someone who "doesn't work" has nothing interesting to talk about. They're wrong. A good many full-time moms out there have intellects and interests that match those of anyone on a corporate payroll.

Kathy sometimes feels stuck when she stands there in jeans and a t-shirt to watch me take off for work in a suit, driving the convertible we bought for her in our prechild days. While I'm in my office reading over the morning faxes from Washington, London, and Tokyo, she's in our kitchen trying to get our daughters to eat their breakfast without splattering it all over the walls. While I'm sitting in a corporate conference room with my steaming cup of coffee discussing high-profile business actions, she's arguing with the girls about what clothes they should wear and trying to get them dressed and into the car so they won't be late for nursery school. While I'm in a helicopter on my way to a press conference in Manhattan, she's taking Simone and Bernadette to story hour at the town library.

She spends hours at preschool every week as a helping mother, receiving little recognition, if any. Yet everyone remarks at what a great father I am when I take an afternoon off to attend my daughter's end-of-the-year nursery school party.

Simone and Bernadette lead active, rich, stimulating lives. And Kathy is there to help them do it.

Here's a salute to Kathy, Cheryl, and all the moms who are working so hard to raise our children. Whether they are at home with their kids full time, or achieving the balance between parenting and careers, their mark on the future is incalculable. We owe them.

About the Authors

George Jamison has worked as a journalist, military officer, and international communications manager for a major U.S. company. He is originally from Albany, New York, and is a graduate of Boston University. He lives in Connecticut with his wife, Kathy, and his daughters, Simone, Bernadette, and newly born Caroline. His articles have appeared in the *New York Times* and other newspapers in the Northeast.

Kenneth R. Freeston is an educator in Connecticut where he lives with his wife, Cheryl, and son, David. He has been an assistant superintendent of schools, a principal of a national exemplary school, and a high school teacher of psychology and history. Ken's articles have appeared in the *New York Times.* He frequently serves as a consultant to other school districts and has published articles on instruction and educational leadership in professional journals. He received both a B.A. and a master's degree from Colgate University and a Ph.D. from the University of Connecticut.